Moses Was Watching Over Me

*A memoir of miracles from Arthur Neigut,
a Holocaust survivor*

by Karen Polis and Azriela Jaffe

∞INFINITY
PUBLISHING

Copyright © 2013 by Karen Polis

ISBN 978-0-7414-9892-2 Paperback
ISBN 978-0-7414-9893-9 Hardcover
ISBN 978-0-7414-9894-6 eBook
Library of Congress Control Number: 2013917549

Printed in the United States of America

Published March 2014

INFINITY PUBLISHING
1094 New DeHaven Street, Suite 100
West Conshohocken, PA 19428-2713
Toll-free (877) BUY BOOK
Local Phone (610) 941-9999
Fax (610) 941-9959
Info@buybooksontheweb.com
www.buybooksontheweb.com

Table Of Contents

Acknowledgments

I would like to thank the following people who contributed one way or another to this book:

Joel Polis, who was the inspiration for starting the whole thing.

Brenda Jo Samryk who transcribed the original five-tape interview into a 300-page document.

Azriela Jaffe for creating the framework this book was built on and coming up with the brilliant idea of making each chapter a "miracle."

Carrie Adkins-Ali and Marcia Comstock for providing their editing services.

Joyce Sokolic for meeting with me numerous times during the process, helping with proofreading and providing information, as well as contributing financially.

Jeff and Susie Rabelow for various forms of help, including being extra pairs of eyes during the editing process.

Malcolm and Eleanor Polis for their financial contribution, as well as being extra pairs of eyes during the editing process.

The various people along the way who helped provide information for fact-checking and other aspects of pulling all the pieces of this book together.

And of course, a special thanks to Arthur Neigut for telling his story, for his financial contribution, and for his patience during the making of a book that has been a long time in coming.

Foreword

When I was five years old, I remember my Uncle Arthur reaching his arms out to me, and me climbing onto his lap and sitting there contentedly for a long time. He was characteristically kind and soft spoken, and handsome even as an older man. I never thought to question the "KL" tattooed on the topside of his right wrist, and he never spoke of it. When I was a little older, my parents explained to me that the tattoo was from Arthur's time in a concentration camp during World War II. Arthur has always been very healthy, strong, outgoing, and full of life. I know this contributed to why he survived.

It wasn't until about 1996 that Arthur began to speak of his Holocaust experience when he agreed to participate in Steven Spielberg's Shoah documentary. Eight years later, I interviewed him myself, and had the opportunity to hear his whole story–a story even his two children had never heard in full.

The process of how this book came together is a book in and of itself. Suffice it to say that it started during a family gathering. Arthur was answering a few questions about his experience, mostly posed by my Uncle Joel, who was visiting from California. Joel stated that somebody ought to write these stories down. Then Joel turned to me (knowing my propensity for writing) and said, "Karen, if you don't write a book about this, I will."

Challenge accepted...

To hear Arthur Neigut's voice, go to
www.MosesWasWatchingOverMe.com for
free audio clips from his original interviews.

The Survivors of the Shoah Visual History
Foundation was founded in 1994 by Steven
Spielberg as a way to formally document the
stories of survivors and other witnesses to the
Holocaust. As a registered Holocaust survivor,
Arthur Neigut was interviewed for the Shoah
Foundation in August 1996.

Introduction

I am a statistical miracle: a Jew from Poland who made it out of the war alive. For years, I kept the story to myself, eating away at me inside. The first time I spoke of it was 51 years later when I was interviewed for the Shoah Foundation. But I never told the full story[1]–and I left out the most important part.

In the late 1950s, as I was watching Charlton Heston playing Moses in the now-classic movie "The Ten Commandments," chills began to run through my entire body. I thought back to the camps, and remembered all of the many times that I had felt somebody looking out for me. Suddenly, I was absolutely certain that Moses had to be the one.

The Hebrew prophet Moses liberated the Hebrew slaves from Egypt and led them to Mount Sinai and eventually to the "Promised Land" of Israel. Moses received the Torah from God at the top of Mount Sinai.

At 13 years old, I went from being the baby of a privileged family into Hell. It is a miracle that I'm here today to tell my story–the story of being imprisoned in the concentration camps during World War II, and how Moses was with me the entire time.

Moses, who led the Jewish people out of Egypt, led me out of the camps alive; delivering me from evil. At the time, I did not have a name for the presence that I felt so strongly. I just knew without a doubt that somebody was watching over me—whispering in my ear, sometimes shouting, telling me what to do, showing me where to go, giving me hope and strength, direction and comfort. That presence kept me alive during one of the darkest eras in history—a diabolic manmade nightmare few survived.

Most Orthodox and Conservative Jews observe the dietary practice of keeping Kosher. Based on laws set forth in the Torah, keeping Kosher is a way for observant Jews to obey their God and preserve their Jewish identity. The following are a few of the Kosher laws: Do not eat pork or shellfish; do not eat meat and dairy in the same meal; use a different set of dishes and utensils for meat than those used for dairy.

I'm not a particularly religious man. I never was. I don't keep kosher or go regularly to synagogue or keep the Sabbath; but what I do keep is a strong, unshakable faith that God sent Moses to protect me, and Moses is still with me even today. I'm telling my story now because I want people to know how I survived. I want them to know about Moses.

Miracle 1

God Sent Moses

The Polish Jews came under German rule after the Nazi invasion of Poland on the first of September 1939.

I was born Osiek Neugut (pronounced: Osh-ik Nī-gʊt) on June 13, 1926 in the outer suburbs of Kraków, Poland. As the baby of the family, I received a lot of attention from my older siblings. They helped my parents raise me and spoiled me with candies and trinkets just to see me smile. My childhood home was jovial and loving, filled with the laughter of my beautiful mother and the aromas of her wonderful homemade cooking.

My mother, Niska, was tall and slim with long dark hair and a friendly smile. Intelligent and multi-talented, she did everything from cooking and cleaning to making our clothes, all without the luxury of today's modern conveniences. She could single-handedly create a fabulous spread of delicious food for the entire family and often for guests, too. My mother was vivacious and warm, and people loved being around her.

My father, Kiwa (pronounced: Kēy-va), was a tall, good-looking man with dark hair, a short beard, and a mustache. He had served in the Polish Army in 1918. He was smart and educated and owned a large, successful grocery and meat store. He was also in the money-lending business. Both of my parents were very religious. They kept kosher, they observed the Sabbath, and my father always wore his yarmulke.

My sisters were Sala (who we called Saly) and Erna Esther. Saly looked like a cross between our mother and father. She lived in center city Kraków with her husband, a Polish man who was a member of the Communist Party. Erna lived with us. She had black hair and big blue eyes. Together, my sisters owned a cosmetics store in the city. My brothers were Moniek, Itzhak, and Israel (who we called Srulek, which is the Yiddish nickname for Israel). My brothers and I looked a lot like our mother. Moniek was three years older than I. After school, he helped our father at the grocery store. All of the siblings had the same light complexion and blue eyes, but Moniek had lighter hair than the rest of us. Itzhak was much older, and when I was still just a baby, he left Poland to live out his life in Argentina where we had cousins. I never really knew him. Srulek was about 10 years older than I and had a wholesale business buying live cattle by the trainload and transporting them for sale to various locations. My memory of him is vague. I was still a little boy when Srulek met with a tragic end long before the war began. He was returning home from a business trip one night with a stash of cash when the Polish Mafia robbed and shot him. Perhaps it was merciful— he never had to witness what would become of his family.

We lived in a large, single-level house on a street named Ulica Starowiczna and were one of the few Jewish families in the neighborhood. We had a vegetable garden that I helped tend, and my mother made good use of everything we grew there. We also had a cold room buried in the ground in our backyard, which served as refrigeration. Not far from our house, my father had a warehouse that was part of his business. He would buy a large, wholesale pallet of goods–such as flour and sugar–to sell for retail and store the extras in the warehouse. A small creek ran behind our property, and my friends and I used to go fishing there and turn over stones in search of little critters like frogs and crayfish. I had a medium-sized, mixed-breed dog that I took good care of. His name escapes me now, but I do remember one day when I was walking him, he broke free from his leash and started running. I didn't want to lose him, so I ran faster than the dog and I caught him.

Our family was very well off compared to our neighbors, though our house was only slightly larger than the others on the street. We had a dining room, a living room that included a kitchen, and two bedrooms. One of the bedrooms was huge; big enough to accommodate me and all my siblings. Many families at the time did not have a separate bedroom or even a separate bed for each member of the family. Back then, personal automobiles were a rare privilege, and we were the only family on our street that owned a car. We also had plumbing and electricity, true luxuries of the time. Our family had plenty of money, good food, and warm clothes to protect us from the cold winters. We enjoyed a comfortable, upper-middle class life.

Our kitchen table was large enough to accommodate all of us and then some. My mother was very creative and made the most delicious goulash, brisket, and turkey. For dessert, she often baked one of her many cakes to go with our coffee and fruit. I loved everything my mother made.

> The sacrificial ritual of Kapparah was common among Eastern European Jews and was performed on the eve of Yom Kippur (the Day of Atonement). This ritual consisted of swinging a live chicken three times around one's head while reciting three times in Hebrew: "This be my substitute, my vicarious offering, my atonement. This [chicken] shall meet death, but I shall find a long and pleasant life of peace!"

Because my parents kept kosher, we had separate dishes and silverware for meat and for dairy, and we had three sets of dishes: everyday china dishes, holiday dishes, and Passover dishes. Holidays were very special. Our extended family and many of our neighbors, both Jewish and Gentile, came to join us. To celebrate the first day of Passover, we had a big Seder, and my father made matzos in our oven. I remember Rosh Hashanah with a table full of family and delicious meals and desserts emerging from my mother's kitchen. Before Yom Kippur, my mother would swing a live chicken around her head and light the Yom Tov candles.

Even on regular days, it was not unusual to have relatives stop by to join us for dinner and sometimes spend the night. Often, they came out of need, and my parents were generous with their financial help as well as their meals. There was always plenty of food from the grocery business, and we were happy to host many parties. It was a lively and loving atmosphere and a close family.

The Sabbath was a holy day of rest, and even small acts of maintaining a household were prohibited, so my parents hired a Gentile woman to come to our home each Saturday so that we could have light, heat, and food. This was common practice among Polish Orthodox Jews. My mother would prepare a different meal every Friday, and the woman would come on Saturday to light the oven and cook the prepared food.

My parents followed many religious rituals. They walked to synagogue every Saturday and had prayer books at home from which they would pray several times a day. They were strict about keeping kosher and fasted on Yom Kippur. They celebrated every Jewish holiday in the proper tradition.

I, on the other hand, showed no interest in religion. The only reason I ever went to synagogue was to hear the shofar being blown on Rosh Hashanah, the Jewish New Year. All the kids liked the shofar. The religious men would duel to see who could hold a note the longest and loudest, and in between, the congregation would chant the prayers. At the very end, each man would take a big breath and blow an extra long note.

I did not pray and I certainly did not fast. Nor did I keep kosher. In fact, I sometimes ate meals at the homes of my Gentile friends. One day, the priest even invited me to lunch at his church. My parents let me get away with all of it, and I never felt the need to hide anything from them. My parents were good-natured and loving, and since I was the youngest, they found it hard to say no to me.

The local merchants all knew me. (I'm guessing some of them also had loans out with my father.) I could stop in their stores and ask for candies or other small items and tell them that my mother would pay for it later. The storeowners happily obliged because they knew that my parents were able to afford the things I asked for. My family was well known in the neighborhood and well liked.

As a kosher family, we were not allowed to eat pork. Positively not. That didn't stop me from enjoying kielbasa on a regular basis. Just a couple blocks away, there was a butcher that specialized in kielbasa. My friends and I would sometimes pass by the smokehouse and see the fresh meat dripping with juices, and smell the enticing aroma. The butcher would give us each a big piece of kielbasa for free. It was delicious–I didn't care that it wasn't kosher.

In 1939, I was in the eighth grade. Most Jewish parents sent their children to a Jewish day school, but I attended a regular public school along with all of my neighborhood friends. Each evening, I would sit at the kitchen table and do an hour or so of homework, and my brother Moniek would help me out whenever he could. School wasn't too hard, and I didn't mind going.

Hebrew school was another story. The teacher was scary! He was a very strict Rabbi with an unpleasant, severe look on his face. The first day, the Rabbi taught us how to pray. My parents did plenty of that, and I already knew I wasn't interested. Just one day of Hebrew school was enough for me. I went home and told my mother how much I hated it, and she did not make me go back.

Though I was off the hook for Hebrew school, I would be turning 13 soon, and my parents insisted that I have a bar mitzvah. They could teach me whatever I needed to know for the ceremony, and I would be expected to read from the Torah in perfect Hebrew in front of all my family and friends. I dreaded it! My parents were very much looking forward to this important milestone. They would be so proud to watch their little boy inducted into manhood. Nobody knew then that not only would I become a man in the eyes of the Jewish community, but my childhood was about to be ripped out from under me, and a 13-year-old boy would be forced to grow up overnight.

I had no fun going to a day of Hebrew school, but I had a lot of fun every year helping my friends decorate their Christmas trees. Their moms would bake these big, special Christmas cookies, and we kids would wrap the cookies in different colors of foil and hang them on the tree along with the lights. I was even invited to the home of one of my friends for a delicious Christmas dinner.

All of my friends lived in my neighborhood, so after dinner, we would all meet outside to play. We would walk to the local candy store, play ball, climb trees, and make up our own games. We were typical active and carefree young boys. On rainy nights, I would stay home and play cards with Moniek, while my parents would sit with us in the living room and talk. Once in a while, the whole family would go to the movies; a rare and special treat.

On certain days, my father would drive into the city to buy wholesale meat for his store from a huge open market where livestock were auctioned off. He took me along because he knew I enjoyed the adventure. The auction and market made a big impression on me with all of the noise and confusion, and with my father right in the midst of things: shouting out numbers, haggling to get the best price, and exchanging money. He would bid on whatever he needed for his business, like cattle, sheep, and goats. Of course, he never bid on any of the pigs! Later, the animals would be slaughtered and the meat delivered to his store.

My second cousin, Max Neugut, lived in a neighboring town, and he and his wife would visit us about once a month. Max was a short, unattractive man with an aggressive personality. He liked me very much and I liked him. He always brought a small gift for me, usually some candies from his business. (He had two wholesale businesses: one in candy and the other in fabric.) My father used to help him out quite a bit, providing him with free business advice. Max kept up with all of the latest political goings-on, and war became the main topic of conversation. The newspapers and radio brought us news of the German Army advancing and what they were doing to the Jews in Germany. As soon as the Nazis descended on Poland, Max joined an underground movement and was able to escape the occupation of his town and survive the war through those channels.

I was lucky not to have much direct experience with the growing anti-Semitism throughout Poland. Only once did I have a run-in with one of my schoolmates. He was a big kid and did not live in my neighborhood. I hardly knew him. One day, on the school playground, he started taunting me, "You Jews go back to Palestine–that's where you belong!" I told him, "I'm not going to fight. My brother will take care of you." So the next day, Moniek waited for him after school and beat him up. That kid did not bother me anymore.

When it came time to have my bar mitzvah, the Nazis were close enough that the scary Rabbi from Hebrew school knew it wasn't a good idea to draw attention. The synagogue could not risk a great display of Judaism. What was meant to be a big affair, full of family and friends, turned out to be just my parents and a few others with a piece of cake and some wine. I had not studied anything, so I only read a tiny bit of Hebrew, and that was it. When my father congratulated me, his eyes did not shine from pride, but from the tears of a profound, unspoken sadness. I didn't think much of it; I was just glad I didn't have to speak in front of a large audience.

The first time I really understood how close the Germans were was when our relatives from the city came to our house. My sister Saly and her husband, and my mother's sister and her three children, all came together, leaving their homes and almost all of their possessions behind. The German Army had just invaded Poland. Nobody knew what would happen when they reached Kraków, but my relatives were not going to stick around to find out.

Saly and her husband came just to tell us goodbye. Because her husband was a communist, the Soviet Union would allow them into its borders, so the two of them had a chance to escape. "Maybe we'll see you," they said, "we hope...when the war is over."

My aunt and cousins came to live with us. It was fun having them there. For me, the more people, the better. After dinner, we would all go into the living room to listen to the radio and have some cake and tea. The news was full of accounts of how the Jews in Germany were being restricted from living their regular lives, and the general consensus in our family was: "When the Germans get over here, we're going to be in bad shape." The discussions around the household concerning the war were very open. Nobody tried to shelter me from it, but I did not understand; I was too young to believe anything like that could really be true.

A recent letter from relatives in the United States offered us a safe haven. (My father's two sisters, Fannie and Nettie, and his brother, Albert, had moved to America many years before along with some cousins on my mother's side.) My parents considered the offer, but decided to stand their ground and see what would happen. Everybody was hoping for the best, and there were too many of us to try to escape to another country. We would have had to break the family up into smaller units, and we didn't want to do that. Everybody was afraid, and we felt safer staying together.

The Polish Army drove through our street shouting, "They're coming! The Germans are coming! We're going to fight them." But we didn't need this announcement to know that the Germans had arrived in center city Kraków. When we stepped outside our house we could hear them off in the distance, shooting.

By this time, anti-Semitism was rampant in Poland, and the media reports were full of people saying, "All you Jews go to Palestine. That's the only way you're going to be saved. Just leave and go to Palestine." Many Polish citizens were happy that the German Army was coming to rid Poland of all the Jews.

In our neighborhood, people went about their daily business. My family was still keeping the Sabbath sacred, my father was still going to work, and I was still going out after dinner to play. (My non-Jewish friends and I were too young to feel any difference between us.) Even though everyone kept up a semblance of normalcy, the mood around the neighborhood grew solemn. Everybody, both Gentile and Jewish alike, was anxious to know what was going to happen, and it was all happening so fast.

My family was listening to the radio for every move the German Army was making. We thought maybe we would have a month to get out of there, but the Nazi war machine moved much faster than anybody imagined. It only took a week for the Germans to go from Kraków to our street. We could hear them coming. They came marching in with their red armbands, helmets, and machine guns. They marched in rows of four that seemed to go on for at least a mile. Some of them came on horses, some in tanks, some in cars. Most of them came on foot. The occupation happened all in one day. They marched in and took over everything. After that, there was nothing we could do–escape was no longer an option.

The Germans occupied whatever empty spaces they could find. We heard a commotion in our yard, and when we went to see what was going on, the soldiers were making room for themselves in our warehouse. They told us, "From now on, this belongs to us." They took over whatever they wanted, and our ample warehouse was the main place that they stayed on the whole street. They must have thought it was quite a find! They set up shop in there with their own kitchen and all their supplies. Even though the German government was feeding them, the soldiers also used a lot of our stored food. They took over our cold cellar as well.

We continued to live in our house, but as soon as the occupation occurred, the Jews were no longer allowed to go to public school, Hebrew school, or synagogue. My father could no longer go to work. With his beard and ever-present yarmulke, he was conspicuously Jewish, and he kept himself hidden away inside the house. The neighborhood's atmosphere became quiet and fearful. Everybody started talking amongst themselves, wondering, "What is going to happen next?" At some point, the German soldiers came into our home and said, "You are Jews, aren't you? You are not going to be able to live here much longer; you will be going to a ghetto." They told us we would have a place to work at the ghetto and promised us many things that didn't sound so bad; things that never happened.

Our non-Jewish neighbors were all afraid, and they stopped associating with us. They knew that the Jews would be relocated to ghettos, but they did not know what was going to happen to them, and they weren't taking any chances. In those days, there was a lot of guessing. Nobody could imagine the full horror of what would eventually come to pass.

During the occupation, we were still allowed to leave our house to visit neighbors or go to the store. Money was not a concern—our family had plenty of savings and our relatives from the city were wealthy and had brought their money with them. What was a concern was seeing the German troops patrolling up and down our street, day and night. The whole neighborhood was reluctant to pass by the soldiers, so we mostly stayed inside our houses or close to our own yards. I still went out to play, but only with my immediate next-door neighbors. All my family members agreed that it was best to stay nearby so we could keep track of one another and not worry, wondering what might happen if we were out of each others' sight.

We had so many German soldiers staying on our property it was almost impossible not to mix with them. I got along well with the soldiers, and they liked me because I was a child; and with my blue eyes, tall stature, and fine bone structure, they probably did not realize I was Jewish. They gave me things to eat, patted me on the back, and greeted me with, "Guten Tag!" I was the youngest in my household and had always been spoiled. I had never been exposed to anything negative, so I had no reason to dislike the Nazis. I was treated well by them right up until the moment we were ordered to go to the ghetto. I didn't know that they were devils.

I watched from my front yard as the German soldiers celebrated their capture of Kraków. They were drinking and carrying on. I heard the Captain yelling ferociously at one of his men, and I saw him pull out his gun. I went back into the house then, not wanting to see what was next. The following day, I was told that the soldier had done something wrong and the Captain had shot him. I thought to myself, "Well, he must've done something pretty bad." After all, what did I know about war and how things were handled in the military?

One night, a couple of weeks into the occupation, my sister Erna Esther did not come home. It was a miserable night. Everybody was worried, suspecting the worst. Our fears were confirmed when somebody came and told us that she had been killed by the Nazis. Nobody knew why or how, and nobody had seen it happen, but somehow we knew for sure that she was dead. Probably, her death had something to do with her cosmetics business; maybe she went to retrieve valuables from the store and refused to hand them over to the Nazis. Though I knew Erna had been murdered, I still did not really understand what was going on. Our household was filled with a horrible, horrible feeling. I had never seen my parents cry like that. There was nothing they could do to ease their grief. They would never see their daughter again–not even her dead body, and there would be no funeral to say goodbye to her. On top of everything, we knew that Saly and her husband had left the country, but we had no way to know if they had made it safely to the Soviet Union, or if they too had been murdered.

I don't know how long the occupation lasted–maybe a couple of weeks, maybe a month–but my parents were still grieving when we were sent to the ghetto. The Germans only gave us a couple of days' notice. By then, they had already taken inventory of how many people were in each house, and they had a list of every Jewish person who was to go to the ghetto. The army put signs around the neighborhood telling us the date we needed to be ready by and giving us instructions. We were allowed to bring only what we could carry. We packed up clothes, jewelry, and a little bit of food. Everything else had to be left behind.

The day we were leaving, the German soldiers came by with their list to check that everybody was in the house. They went down our street, entering each Jewish household and shouting, "'Raus mit dir! 'Raus mit dir!" (Get out!). I put my dog out in the yard to run free, gave him plenty of food, and hoped one of my Gentile neighbors would take care of him.

It was a beautiful autumn morning when the Nazis loaded us onto the open backs of their army trucks, shouting at us in harsh German. We knew they meant business. My mother and father, my brother, my aunt, my three cousins, and I all climbed onto the truck with our bags. I was confused. Up until then, the soldiers had been so nice to me. I would not understand what was happening until I actually got to the ghetto. Only then would I understand what the adults had been talking about all along. Suddenly, it would all make sense.

Miracle 1: God sent Moses to watch over me.

I had never learned about Moses as a child, so how could I ever guess that he would become my personal protector in the brutal years that lay before me.

When the war was over, I did not want to think about what had happened to me, so I chose to forget. I even convinced myself that large parts of my experience were now lost forever, somewhere in my mind. The funny thing is, when I'm sitting by myself and all is silent, I can picture everything as if I were back there.

What I remember most are those extraordinary moments when I knew beyond a doubt, that somebody was watching over me. Now, I want my children and grandchildren to hear how Moses intervened to keep me alive against all odds.

At the age of thirteen, though I wouldn't realize it until years later, God sent Moses to look after me in the camps and keep me safe. Despite all the cruelty and loss during those six years, I feel that my life is truly blessed. Moses was always close by me, and I believe he always will be until I pass from this earth.

During 1940 and 1941 most of the Jews in Poland were relocated out of their homes and forced into overcrowded, filthy ghettos.

Food was in scarce supply in the ghettos, and even a potato peel could be called a meal. From the beginning, Jews were sneaking out of the ghettos to smuggle food back in, in a lucrative black market.

While German Nazi soldiers guarded the exterior perimeter of ghettos and concentration camps, within the fences, members of the Jewish Order Service were in charge. Many of these "Jewish police" became corrupt and treated their fellow Jews no better than did the Nazis.

When the ghettos were "liquidated," all of the residents were sent to Auschwitz or other death camps for immediate extermination.

Moses Was Watching Over Me

Miracle 2

Finding Emotional Strength

My family and I rode silently on the back of the truck, while my mind was full of thoughts; wondering what a "ghetto" would be like. I looked over the railing at the short caravan of military vehicles flanked by German police on motorcycles and horses, carting my Jewish neighbors.

After several hours, we arrived at the main gate to the Zakliczyn[2] ghetto. Our truck was surrounded by viciously barking dogs, German soldiers with guns, and Jewish ghetto police wearing their identifying armbands–a white band with a blue Star of David. Barbed wire surrounded long stretches of dismal buildings. My first sight of our new residence gave me a very bad feeling. I did not even know what a ghetto was, but I knew that something terrible was going to happen.

Living at Zakliczyn in the cramped quarters of our second-floor apartment felt like being in jail. There was nothing to do and nowhere to go. We didn't even have a deck of cards to occupy our time, and nobody wanted to step foot outside the apartment and risk a run-in with the Jewish police. One of our Gentile neighbors who was particularly fond of me, somehow managed to bring food to us in the ghetto.

Less than a week into our stay, before we had a chance to establish a new routine, the Jewish police made an announcement on behalf of the soldiers stationed outside the barbed fencing: "Do any of the young people here want to go to work?" They were looking for volunteers, and my parents spoke to me with an urgency and seriousness I had not seen before: "Osiek, you must volunteer to go to work. I know you are still young, barely a man, and the only thing you've known until now is school. But Osiek, listen to us–the war needs laborers. You will have a better chance to survive if you leave this ghetto and go to a working camp." What could I do but take their advice? Looking into the eyes of my mother and father, I knew there was no other choice. Moniek and I both volunteered. We said our goodbyes right there and climbed onto the army truck waiting outside.

I don't know how it is possible for a mother to send away two sons she loves so much, knowing that she may never see them again. Our mother was willing to sacrifice her need to keep us close for the chance we might survive. Now that I am a parent myself, I can better appreciate how incredibly difficult that must have been for both her and my father. If my parents hadn't pushed me to volunteer that day, I know I would not be here now to tell my story.

At the labor camp, Moniek and I were put to work building a road for a dam. (The German Army was planning to flood the roads below by releasing the dam in the event of an attack.) All day long, we loaded stone after heavy stone, and shovelfuls of gravel and dirt into carts that were wheeled away on rails and emptied by other workers. I had never done anything so hard in my life. Moniek was older and stronger and so, had an easier time of it than I did. After only two days, I wrote a letter to my mother back in the ghetto:

Dear Mom,
I can't stay here anymore. The work is too hard. I'm exhausted and my body hurts. I want to come back to live with you and dad. I don't care what might happen in the ghetto. Please–I can't stand it here!
Love,
Osiek

I sent my mother three letters in three days.

The ghetto had not been so bad in comparison, and I did not think things could get much worse than this. At the time, I could not appreciate the adequate and regular meals I was receiving at the labor camp.

One day, one of the workers was wheeling a cart full of stones down a small hill. The cart began to move faster and faster, and he could not keep up with it. He fell, and somehow, his legs got caught underneath the wheels and were cut off. I had never seen anything so gruesome.

With our hands and shovels and aching backs, my brother and I worked and talked side-by-side. Because I had him, I never really spoke with anyone else. After a long day, I would retire to the barracks with about 100 other workers. I would climb to my top bunk and collapse into a dead sleep.

After a couple of months working in the labor camp, the Germans in charge of the construction of the road came to us and said, "Your families back in the ghetto were all taken to Auschwitz last night. We will drive you to the ghetto, and if there are any personal belongings left that you would like to take, you may do so." Moniek and I climbed onto the truck for the short ride back to Zakliczyn. Maybe our parents had left a message for us to let us know how to get in touch with them.

When we got to the ghetto, the Jewish police were the only people still there. When I walked up the steps into the room that my parents were forced to call home for the last couple of months, I saw a big pot of potato soup sitting on top of the stove, still cooking. My stomach sank. Mom had been in the middle of making dinner when she and my father had been taken away. I did not know exactly what had happened to them, but I knew it must have been something horrible. I reached out to touch the hot pot of soup and walked away without touching anything else. I said to the people who had driven us there, "I don't want anything. Thank you. Take me back to the truck." My brother and I left without taking a thing–without even looking to see if there was anything to take.

A few days later, my cousin Max was able to sneak into the labor camp to tell me what had happened. The camp had no fencing and was only lightly guarded, so Max came on several nights to give me money, food, and news from the underground. He was my only contact with the outside world. He explained that my parents had been removed from the ghetto and transported by train to a place called Auschwitz along with the thousands of other Jews who had lived there. He also explained to me what Auschwitz was, and then I knew for sure that my parents were gone forever.

After that, my heart hurt for a very long time. I could not believe that my parents were no longer alive; that only me and my brother Moniek were left. I was unsure of my sister Saly's fate, I felt no connection to my brother Itzhak since I was so young when he left Poland, and the rest of my family was gone. I kept asking myself, "How can I live now, without my parents?" Every night for six months, I thought about what had happened to them, and I cried and cried and cried.

Until that moment, I had taken all the upheaval in my life in stride. Losing my friends, my schooling, my town, my house, my freedom, and the carefree life of a child–these things were hard, but I was naturally optimistic and flexible and made the best of each circumstance. But losing my parents in this way was unfathomable.

I was not emotionally prepared to be an orphan. I was very attached to my parents, and I depended on them for strength, guidance, and safety. It was not just losing my mother and father, but finding out about their unspeakably cruel end that plummeted me into despair. Max had told me that at Auschwitz, all of the Jews transported from the ghettos had been gassed to death in gas chambers and their dead bodies thrown into a crematorium to be burnt. That knowledge was far more devastating than a 13-year-old boy could handle. I might have died of a broken heart. I had to mature fast.

I kept working for the Germans with Moniek nearby. He was a source of strength for me. Little by little, I was able to overcome my grief. Because I was at the labor camp rather than a concentration camp, I still had enough food, tolerable treatment, and most importantly, my brother by my side. In addition to these blessings,

I believe that Moses surrounded me with love when I needed it most and helped to lift me out of this very dark place.

The scariest thing I remember from the labor camp wasn't seeing somebody's legs get cut off or being forced to endure hour upon hour of exhausting work–it was when I walked all alone through a pitch-black forest in the dead of night to meet my cousin who was no longer willing to risk meeting me at the camp. I walked for six or seven miles, listening to the eerie sounds of a forest at night: owls hooting, mysterious scuffling noises, the rasping sound of crickets. I knew a guard might spot me at any moment. It was a terrifying walk, but I told myself I had to do it to get money and additional food for Moniek and myself.

When it was time to return to the camp, I asked Max if I could stay with him instead, but he told me I was too young–we would be caught. I thought of running away on my own, but to where? To whom? Everyone was gone and there was nowhere to go. I returned to camp. As long as I made it back by 6 AM roll call, I would be okay. I ate some of the food on the walk home and saved the rest for Moniek. It tasted better and was more nutritious than what they were feeding us at the labor camp. I planned to give the money to Moniek to hide in his clothing (our clothes were not inspected at the labor camp as they were in some concentration camps). We both knew if he were to hide the money under his mattress another worker was sure to steal it.

Shortly after my forest walk, two workers tried to escape from the labor camp in the middle of the night. The following morning, from my high vantage point working on the road, I witnessed the consequence of their attempt to escape. Far below me, two armed German guards followed the prisoners, who carried shovels. The prisoners were marched to the edge of the forest where the guards forced them to dig their own graves. Then the guards shot them and covered them up where they fell.

I watched without thinking or feeling much of anything. After the terrible experience of losing my parents, I simply accepted the situation I was in without question, but I never risked leaving the camp again. Looking back, I often wondered: How did I ever manage to walk through the forest at night by myself? My only answer is that I was young and stupid. And maybe Moses had walked beside me to keep me safe.

I must have been at the labor camp for six months to a year. I am not sure exactly, because how can a person keep track of time when he exists like this? When I left, the dam was still not completed. I don't know if it ever was.

Miracle 2: Finding the emotional strength to survive the loss of my parents.

The miracle of my survival goes far beyond the physical. It is truly incredible that I could emerge from the depths of grief and from what many consider the single greatest atrocity in human history, and go on to experience love, friendship, and joy in life. It would have been understandable if I had left the camps bitter, damaged, and shut down—unable to be emotionally close to another person. But that is not what happened. Moses not only watched over my physical survival, but I believe he also helped me to rebound from the loss of my parents and to heal my heart.

Turns out that the good-natured, friendly child that I was before the war never truly left me. After the war, my life was filled with many blessings, and every day, my best revenge is my smile.

Mielec concentration camp included a Heinkel airplane factory. The inmates who worked at the factory were tattooed with the letters "KL" in blue ink on the top of their right wrists. The letters stood for Konzentrationslager ("Concentration Camp" in German). The airplane workers were valuable to the Nazi cause, and the KL tattoo was intended to set them apart from the regular prisoners. It was a brand that would be easily spotted if any of them tried to escape.

It is commonly thought that every prisoner during the Holocaust received some kind of identifying tattoo (usually a sequence of numbers), but this was only the case at Auschwitz. On the other hand, all inmates at all of the concentration camps were given a cloth number to be sewn onto their uniforms. Using a number, rather than a name, was one of many ways the Nazis dehumanized the prisoners, making it even easier for the Nazis to kill the prisoners without remorse.

Mielec concentration camp was evacuated in May 1944, when the Russian army got too close for comfort.

Miracle 3

A Suitable Job

At the labor camp, an announcement was made that all the laborers were to be transported to Mielec, Poland. Again, I found myself on the back of a truck, this time with standing room only. There was a Heinkel airplane factory at Mielec and the labor camp workers were being sent there to build warplanes for the German Army.

Mielec was a concentration camp, and my arrival there marked the end of any small freedoms I'd had. At Mielec, we were stripped of our scanty belongings and given striped prison uniforms. Shoes were lined up by size, and we each picked out a pair we thought would fit. A wire fence surrounded the camp. Nazi guards armed with machine guns were stationed at lookout towers just beyond the fence, around the perimeter. Just like at the ghetto, Jewish police kept us in line from the inside.

Our first day there, the Jewish police gave us an orientation which included the location of the washrooms, what time we were expected to line up for meals, and a warning not to get near the fence because it was electrified. If any of us had doubts about the power of the fence, they were banished just a week or two later. Some of the guards would patrol on horses during the day, and at night they would turn the horses loose inside the camp to graze on the grass. One morning, I saw two of those beautiful animals lying dead on the ground where they had grazed too close to the wires. When I saw that, I got sick just watching those mounted guards. It was not the only time that happened. The Nazis didn't care about their horses; they didn't care about anything.

The electric fence was a psychological hardship, but the real problem at Mielec was the lack of adequate food. There was never enough, and we were always hungry.

We were fed only twice a day–a noontime lunch and a midnight dinner. All of the prisoners alternated weekly between working day and night shifts, so rather than feeding breakfast to half the camp one week and the other half the next, breakfast simply was not served. Meals were always the same: watered-down black coffee, thin potato soup, and a small piece of bread. Now and then, in addition to the soup, we would get a horsemeat-salami sandwich. I suspect this must have come from the horses that were electrocuted. It was the most nourishing food we got. Other than potatoes, we were never given any vegetables or even a single piece of fruit. Everything was tasteless, and there was just enough food to keep us alive. I ate everything I was given immediately so that nobody could steal it from me.

At Mielec, I was tattooed[3] on the top of my right arm, just above my wrist, with the letters "KL" for "Konzentrationslager." The work we were doing at the airplane factory was important, and our tattoos were "special" to reflect this. This way, if we tried to escape, they would know to whom we belonged.

The tattooing process was very painful. A German guard took a needle and began jabbing it into my arm, a quarter-inch below the skin. After the war, I consulted with a few different doctors to see if I could have the KL removed, but they said it is too deep. I would have to go through the whole removal process and still would have a big scar. The truth is, I hardly notice it; but subconsciously, I know it's there.

Each day, I would walk the short distance from the sleeping barracks to the airplane factory. I didn't know anything about airplanes, but I knew if I wanted to survive, I'd better learn fast. As it turned out, building airplanes was something I excelled at!

The factory was huge and consisted of various stations for assembling different parts of the plane. My station was for the wings. It took many pieces of aluminum to assemble one wing. Each piece had to be heated to the right temperature to bend it into shape. Riveting the sheets of thin metal together was a precise and tricky process. After heating the rivets, I used an air hammer to get them to lie flush against the holes while another worker held the aluminum sheet for me to keep it still. If any air got in through the holes, it would destroy the wing when the plane took off. I also had to be very careful that the air hammer hit the rivet and not the aluminum sheet, or the whole sheet would be ruined. The German inspector would come by and put a mirror up inside the hollow tube of the wing to see that my rivets were exactly right. They always were.

It took an entire day to complete a pair of wings, which was the only part of the plane I worked on during my stay at Mielec. The wings were built first, and then at other stations within the factory, the body of the plane was built, and then the interior. The final station was for spray painting. To finish an entire plane took about a week. After the war, whenever I would pass a paint store or a place where metal was being heated, the smell would bring memories of the factory at Mielec flooding back to me.

I took to this job very quickly and easily. I was lucky. Whatever somebody guided me to do, I was able to do it without messing up. I learned my job in just two weeks, and within another two months, I was put in charge of six other prisoners to teach them how to do it. All of the prisoners were Polish Jews like myself, so there was no language barrier. Even the German supervisors would speak to us in Polish.

The first six prisoners I was in charge of weren't very good at their jobs. I told my supervisor, "I can't work with these people. They're going to ruin everything." Those six were replaced with experienced workers, and I was happy with them. I never saw the original crew again. I was still new to the workings of a concentration camp, so I had no idea that telling my supervisor my charges were not doing a good job probably got them killed. It would not be too much longer before I realized what went on at the concentration camps.

During the three years I spent at Mielec, my work schedule alternated between one week of day shift and one week of night shift. Shift work is hard enough, never really having time to adjust to each schedule, but with little food to fuel me, it was extra trying. It was also difficult to have an appetite at midnight when dinner was served. Everything tasted sour. The biggest problem with the night shift was that lunch was served during the day while I was sleeping. There were at least a dozen times I was too tired to get in the lunch line in time to get some food. By the time I dragged my weary body out of the barracks, the food was all gone. I had to suffer until the next meal.

Malnourishment created a host of problems among inmates. One day, I had a bad toothache, so I got permission to see the camp dentist rather than go to work. He did not bother to evaluate the tooth, but simply pulled it out with nothing to dull the pain. It hurt terribly-so much that I never went back to the dentist for anything again. The next time I had a toothache, I just endured it until it went away on its own. Other than that one time at the dentist, I went to work every day, sick or not-by now I knew: I had better go to work if I want to stay alive.

Physically, my work was not very demanding. It was nothing compared to the labor camp I had come from. But at least at the labor camp there had been enough food. Mentally, the airplane work was challenging and there was no room for error. Those who couldn't produce were taken to a nearby cemetery and shot. There were no second chances-one mistake and you were gone. Most of the prisoners had never seen a plane in their lives, and quite literally, they could not build a plane to save their lives. They didn't have the ability to pick it up as I did. In truth, I had never seen a plane either, but I had the gift of a budding draftsman and designer to look at the various parts and be able to envision the final product.

I definitely had a feel for this type of work, though I didn't realize then that I would be using these same skills later in my career life. I found the work interesting (much more so than building the road), but still, I had no choice in the matter. I knew the only way to survive was to do a good job, and the extreme stress of that situation made it impossible to have any feelings or perspective around it. I worked, not in exchange for pay or for pride, but in exchange for my life.

The German foreman, manager, and inspector of the airplane factory all saw that I did a very good, clean job for them. They were nice to me and would share some of their food, bringing me an extra sandwich or more soup. This went a long way to help me stay alive. I don't know if the other workers ever suspected this special treatment, but I made sure to eat my food quickly and privately.

The German soldiers outside of the factory were nothing like those with whom I worked closely inside the factory. The ones on the outside were compassionless brutes. The real Nazis were even worse than the Nazis you see in the movies; much worse. If we didn't line up properly for meals, they would hit us with a stick. They would beat, or even shoot someone for the smallest infraction. To me, they were not even human beings. Of course, I had Moses protecting me, so at Mielec, I was never hit with a stick or beaten. I always had Moses to tell me where to go, how to stand, what to do... I was still a child–somebody had to tell me.

One day, while standing in line for food, the inmates were all gossiping about an incident that had occurred the day before among the commanders-in-charge. For the whole camp, there was just one German commander on the outside of the camp who was in charge of the German soldiers, and one Jewish commander on the inside who was in charge of the Jewish police who overlooked the prisoners. A new Jewish commander had recently replaced the current one. The German commander did not like the new guy, so he took him to the cemetery and shot him dead.

Despite all the talk over that incident, nobody really made friends because everybody was just existing. People kept to themselves unless they had a relative with them. At night, when we'd retire to our barracks, the Jewish police would give the "lights out" order, and then we all just went to sleep. No one whispered to each other across the dark. Each day was a very long day. Each night I was dead tired. I went to sleep beneath the single blanket we were given, and sometimes I had dreams in which I could not believe where I was and what type of atmosphere I was in. It was dreadful. But mostly I would sleep so deeply, I don't remember dreaming at all. And forget about daydreaming–there was no psychological room for that. At work, I didn't have a chance to daydream because I was under extreme stress being watched by the foreman, manager, and inspector. I had to concentrate fully on what I was doing and make the right decisions because if not, I'd be killed.

Even when I was eating, I had to fully concentrate just on eating. Every moment was intense; like being in a state of emergency 24 hours a day, seven days a week. We worked eight-hour days, breaking only for our meager meal. During night-shift weeks, there was some downtime between our midnight dinner and our 4 AM bedtime, but I don't remember what I did then, because there was nothing to do. During day-shift weeks, bedtime was immediately after dinner.

There was no time to think, to even consider, any possibility other than my immediate reality. No time to wish I was back at the labor camp eating a sandwich with my brother or back home with my family or anyplace else. I was just surviving day to day–seeing only what was in front of me at the moment and doing whatever it took to still be alive at the end of each day. I don't know how many died at Mielec. Because of the shiftwork, it was hard to talk to people to find out what was happening. When I noticed that someone was missing, that's how I knew they were dead. For the most part, I did not engage with others unless it was to instruct them on building plane wings.

I knew Moniek was here somewhere because he had been with me on the truck from the labor camp, but he did not work at the airplane factory. Because he was tall and strong, they must have needed him for heavier work. Mielec was very large and we could not move about the camp freely, so I didn't see him there. After we were transported from the labor camp, I never saw him again.

Every day and every night, I thought, "I don't know how long I can survive this type of existence. In the next day or so, probably I'll be dead anyway." I wanted to give up because I saw so many people dying all around me. They were older and they could not tolerate these conditions. Back at the ghetto, the German Army had accepted anyone who was willing and able to go to work. Though I was young, I was tall for my age, so I had been accepted. At Mielec, there were a few others who were also very young and worked in the factory with me, but almost everybody was older than I. Most of them just gave up. Why shouldn't I do the same? But I never did give up. With Moses looking out for me, I found the strength to keep going.

What I saw and lived through can never be described in words. It's no wonder that I prefer to forget because I was a young boy forced to grow up fast, and because much of what I experienced was a living nightmare. When I think back on this whole time, it is unbelievable that a human being could survive what I went through. If it wasn't for Moses, I'm sure I would not have survived.

Miracle 3: I was given a suitable job.

I believe Moses saw to it that the right job was given to me–an important job inside a warm factory where I would be given extra food and my life valued for the service I provided. A job that suited my talents and personality. A job that would keep me alive.

As part of Hitler's "Final Solution," the infamous labor and extermination camp of Auschwitz-Birkenau was established with the specific intent of killing masses of people quickly. It was the largest of the camps set in Poland and had several gas chambers and crematoria to carry out its mission. According to the United States Holocaust Memorial Museum in Washington, D.C.: *"At the height of the deportations, up to 6,000 Jews were gassed each day at Auschwitz."* For Jews and other prisoners, transportation to Auschwitz-Birkenau meant almost certain death.

A handful of individuals brought to Auschwitz became part of the labor force, to live a few more days or months in torturous conditions. Hundreds of thousands more went straight from the cattle cars to their deaths.

Miracle  4

Spared At Auschwitz

At Mielec, a German officer announced over the loudspeaker that the Russians were closing in on Poland, and the entire camp would be evacuated. My fellow factory workers and I were told that since we were valuable mechanics, we would be taken to a camp in Germany to continue working on airplanes. The German soldiers loaded all of the inmates onto a cattle train and we began our journey.

The train rambled long into the night before coming to a stop. I peered through the slats of the cattle car and saw the iron sign that, even today, reads, "ARBEIT MACHT FREI" (Work Makes One Free). We had all heard about that sign many times prior to this. Our train had stopped at the dreaded Auschwitz. We all knew what that meant. The crematoriums at Auschwitz worked around the clock, consuming the majority of those who entered the gates–my parents had been among them.

"This is it–this is the end," we said to each other from inside the train. The inevitable end. I wasn't even surprised or scared. I had lived for so long now in a constant state of intense stress, I just accepted whatever came my way–even death.

I had accepted everything in the months after finding out that my mother and father had been murdered in the Auschwitz gas chambers. When everybody is gone, you don't have much to live for. Still, when I was at Mielec, there had been a part of my brain thinking, "If I do the right thing, there's a possibility that I'll survive." But I knew there would be no surviving Auschwitz.

They kept us on the train for a full day and late into the night with no food or water. The train was hot and crowded with standing room only and buckets for bathrooms. Women and children were crying. People were passing out around me. Many people died. The prisoners in my boxcar were trying to help one another, but it was difficult to even move from the spots we were in because the whole train was overloaded. An unfamiliar and revolting smell infiltrated my nostrils. There are a lot of things I no longer remember from my time in the camps, but the smell wafting from the crematoriums into our boxcar is something I will never forget. It was the worst thing I've ever smelled. There had been no crematorium at Mielec, so up until now, I had been spared this overwhelming stench. I was stuck on that hot train with that awful smell for what felt like an eternity. But I had the better end of the deal; all the inmates who did not work with the airplanes were sent off the train, most likely straight to the gas chambers.

Finally, sometime during the night, the train started to move. A silent relief fell over those of us who were left, and again we began to talk quietly. Where would we end up when we got to Germany and what might happen to us?

Miracle 4: I never got off the train at Auschwitz.

I survived Auschwitz by never entering the gates at all. And I was only a few hundred feet away.

I was given another chance to stay alive. Was Moses looking over that train? I know he was.

Miracle 5

Saved By A Sandwich

The Nazi network of facilities for imprisonment, slave labor, containment, extermination, and other purposes was much larger than Holocaust scholars previously believed. The latest information reveals that 42,500 Nazi ghettos and camps have been documented throughout Europe.

I watched Auschwitz get farther and farther away as the train trundled down the tracks. We were on our way to a camp in Germany that housed another airplane factory. It would take a variety of successive camps, including Bergen-Belsen and Treblinka, to get there. Were we on the road for several weeks or several months? I cannot recall, as an even greater lack of food during that time left me with little energy to think.

These camps were all worse than Mielec because, save for one very small camp, they each had a crematorium burning dead bodies. The stench I had first encountered on the train at Auschwitz was now a constant reminder of the extraordinary horror I was somehow living through. The food they served us at each of these camps was about the same as at Mielec–not much of anything–but without the extra sandwiches for a job well done, I was truly starving to death.

Historians often talk about which camps were worse than others, but to me there was not much difference–one was as bad as the other. My life at these transitional camps was a blur of slave labor, constant hunger, watching prisoners succumb to starvation, disease, exhaustion, and assault, and not knowing if I would be alive tomorrow. Up until then, I had carried with me, always in the back of my mind, the thought that I would somehow survive. Now that death surrounded me daily and I had much less food to sustain me, I became fixated on how I was going to die. That was the main problem I had to cope with from day to day because I knew everybody was dying, everybody was shot, everybody was burned... I just didn't want to suffer when my turn came.

Upon arrival at each camp, the prisoners were ordered to get into one of the lines that formed, each for a different job. A Nazi soldier would point and that's where you had to go–no questions asked. Each time, a voice in my head told me which line to get into and because of that voice most of the jobs I ended up with were not too difficult. I would jump from line to line, short enough to escape detection. Moses must have been watching over me because I was never caught.

One of the camps I was in was so small that it had no Jewish police. Nazis guarded from inside the boundaries of the camp rather than outside. In addition to the usual machine guns, these soldiers carried hand grenades with wooden handles that could be turned to activate the grenade. The soldiers yelled at us, "If you don't do what I say, I'm going to throw this grenade at you!" There were no bunks at this camp. We slept in some kind of barn on the cold dirt floor. I was freezing at that place—I don't remember having even so much as a blanket to buffer the cold. Luckily, I was only there for a night because I was part of the select group, the airplane mechanics, who were kept moving from camp to camp, leaving the resident prisoners behind.

I don't know how many other camps in Poland we stayed at before we crossed the border into Germany and stopped at a camp with a sign on the front gate: "Bergen-Belsen." It was here that one of the guards kicked me in the face because I was standing in the back during roll call and could not hear when my number was called. I bled all down the front of my neck. I still have a scar under my chin from that day.

I was put to work digging a tunnel through a mountain. There were people of all different nationalities there: Italian, French, Russian, American, and German political prisoners. It was the first time I worked with people other than Jewish Poles. We shoveled dirt and carried it out of the tunnel in wheelbarrows with everyone speaking different languages. Nobody understood each other—they would just point and shout in their own language, "Do this. Do that." It was miserable, but I only had to put up with it for a short time before we finally moved on to our intended destination.

> Early in the war, the main industry for labor at Flossenbürg concentration camp was a local stone quarry. In 1943 and 1944 labor shifted to the aircraft industry as the Messerschmidt company had established a production plant at the camp.
>
> Messerschmidt had the first operational jet fighter, the ME 262. Despite this advantage, the German Army had several factors working against them. Many of these planes were destroyed by allied bombing while on the ground; lack of fuel meant only a limited number of them could fly at any one time; and some prisoners who worked in the airplane factories would risk their lives by deliberately sabotaging the Nazi planes.

When we arrived at Flossenbürg, Germany, the very first thing I saw was the smoke rising from the crematorium. Flossenbürg was a very large concentration camp imprisoning people from many countries. Almost half the camp consisted of political prisoners.

After a day or so of the typical orientations, I was again sent to work at an airplane factory inside the camp, working one week day shift and one week night shift, just like at Mielec. This time I was building Messerschmitt jet fighter planes. Jet planes were a new invention at the time. The Germans were the first to fly them in combat, and I was among the first to build them.

The routine here was the same as at the other camps, but the food at Flossenbürg was the worst of all. The coffee tasted like dishwater, the bread was always stale, and the soup was watery. There was no substance to give us nourishment, and there was never enough. The German Army was fed first. If there was any horsemeat left over that day, it would go to the prisoners; otherwise we just got bread and soup.

When I had been at Mielec, I had not witnessed much death and there had been no crematorium, but at Flossenbürg, death was a daily occurrence. Every morning, when I went into the bathrooms to wash, I had to step over four or five skeletal corpses to get to the sinks. I could not avoid this because it was mandatory to get washed in the morning before work, and the bodies were not collected for burning until later in the day. That was the most horrible thing about Flossenbürg, but walking over those bodies quickly came to mean nothing to me. They could have been books rather than bodies lying there. It's unbelievable what a person can get used to.

On Saturdays, there was a place to go to take a shower and then get clean clothes from a big pile and get a different pair of shoes. After the shower, a guard would tell me that there were women available for sex, but I never wanted to be with any of them. The clothes were always the same, regardless of the season. We were not given a coat in the wintertime. I remember walking to work in the snow on a path dug by inmates between the barracks, washrooms, and factory. The snow piled along the sides of the path would go down into my shoes because the shoes were too big, and I was walking fast to get out of the cold. I didn't have a coat or undershirt or any fat on my body to keep me warm; just a long-sleeved shirt, a pair of pants, underwear, socks[4], and shoes. Still, it wasn't too bad for me because I didn't have very far to walk from the barracks to the factory, and the factory was always warm. But each morning, we had to line up for roll call outside. During the coldest weather, many people died while waiting for roll call to end.

The prisoners were not the only ones who suffered from the cold. The bathrooms were located close to one of the corners of the camp, and every morning, I could see one of the guards standing at his post, just beyond the electric fence. One snowy day, when the weather was particularly blustery, I watched the guard standing there holding his machine gun, and he was so cold he did not know what to do with himself. I will always remember watching him fiddle with his gun, pretending to shoot it just to keep moving. He was freezing even more than I was because I would spend most of my day inside the warm factory. He had no choice but to stand out there for hours in the bitter, biting wind. Those soldiers did not have it easy either–if they did anything wrong they would probably be shot just as quickly as one of the inmates.

It was almost impossible to escape from Flossenbürg, but during one of my night-shift weeks, a group of a dozen people tried. I was woken in the middle of the day when everybody was ordered to gather at a central location. Here, the attempted escapees were lined up, standing on benches with ropes around their necks. German soldiers pushed the benches out from underneath the prisoners, and we all watched them hang. The Nazis wanted to show us what would happen if we tried to escape. The bodies were kept hanging for two days for everybody to see as we went to and from work. Prisoners were dying daily from disease, hunger, exposure, and being beaten and shot; and yet, it seemed that the Nazis thought the hangings would be seen as a far worse fate to deter us from escaping. I wasn't old enough to figure out how to escape, though I could understand why those twelve people tried.

There were no gas chambers at Flossenbürg (or at any of the camps that I was in), so the guards would shoot people and then throw them into the crematorium at the end of the camp. At one point, they were burning bodies every day. The odor was terrible. All day, every day, and throughout the night you could smell the burning bodies. That smell I never got used to. You cannot get used to it. It was a sickening stench, and part of what made it so sickening was that I knew what they were burning over there.

At the Messerschmitt factory, I was again working on plane wings, and within a short time, I was once again put in charge of six other inmates. One day, the Gestapo general came to inspect the facility and make sure none of the workers were sabotaging the planes. The inspector of the factory called the Gestapo general over, showed him my work and said, "Listen, this Osiek is doing a beautiful job over here." The general clapped me on my shoulder and said to the inspector, "Give him extra soup." As at Mielec, the Germans in charge over me at the factory had already been bringing me some soup, half a sandwich...whatever they could from the German kitchen. Now, with the general's command, I was assured that this would continue. Again, I was spared from being beaten or abused because of my good work. I always tried to keep ahead.

Flossenbürg was no better than any other camp, but it was easier on me. There, I regained my optimism, and more than ever, I had the feeling that someone was watching over me, even though I would not recognize that that someone was Moses until years later. That feeling gave me hope and strength. Because I was still young (I entered Flossenbürg at 18 years old), the conditions didn't affect me the way they affected the older inmates. I was able to withstand the cold and the lack of nourishment. I was a fast learner. I did what I was told to do and did it well, and I got extra food for my efforts. All of these things helped me to survive.

I tried to help the six Jewish fellows who worked for me. They were under constant stress, afraid of what would happen to them if they were not able to do the work, so I tried my best to show them what to do. I remember one time, one of the guys was holding the sheet of wing metal for me so that I could shoot the rivets into it. I yelled at him, "You better hold it right, because if it doesn't go in correctly, you will be dead!" I got so angry at him, but it was just so that he wouldn't be killed.

Trying to help my fellow workers was about the extent of any human connection made in the camps. I do not remember smiling at anyone, exchanging looks or words, or showing other displays of normal humanity. Even praise from my superiors was a source of survival rather than a source of pride. Inside the factory, we were all under so much pressure to do our jobs correctly; outside the factory, we could smell the smoke from the burning bodies. There was never a time that we weren't on high alert.

The German political prisoners who worked in the airplane factory looked up to me even though I was the youngest one there because they knew that I did my job well. They were able to get inside information from talking to the German guards, and they would pass that information on to me. By now I was fluent in German. Even though my six workers were Polish, my native language was starting to fade because we were all too weak to talk. After the war, I eventually lost my German as well, and English became my first language. One day, my German coworkers said to me, "Just do the best you can because the Americans are not too far away. So do a good job and don't try to escape because we will be liberated one of these days."

News of the American Army approaching brought with it a glimmer of hope. Our spirits were lifted. Finally, there was a reason to engage in conversation with my fellow workers. While waiting in line for food or a shower, I started to make friends.

The bombing from American planes during the day was getting closer and more frequent, while English planes were bombing during the night. Sirens blared throughout the camp in response to these nighttime air raids. "Licht aus!" "Licht aus!" came the command from the loudspeakers. "Lights out!" Every light in the factory and throughout the whole camp was turned off so the planes could not spot us from the night air. (By day, it didn't matter if the lights stayed on, so daytime bombings did not interfere with work.) We were told, "Just sit still where you are. Don't move. Don't go anywhere." Inside the darkened factory, all work ceased and the only thing we could do was go to sleep. I found myself a good spot close to my partially built wings and dozed off to the distant sound of bombing. I looked forward to these air raids during my night-shift weeks. The bombing went on all night and gave us a much-needed break from work and a chance to recuperate. From my perspective, the air raids were fantastic.

Work continued on, the same as always, day after day, but as the German enemies got closer there was less and less food available. The foreman and the inspector continued to bring me sandwiches and this kept me going. The Americans and Russians were closing in at the same time from opposite directions. The bombings from the Americans and from the English were now happening every day and every night. The German officers started to talk about moving us to another camp. They wanted to save their valuable airplane mechanics and keep us cranking out their planes. There were a few thousand of us–mostly Jewish, all relatively young, all now excellent mechanics; expert at our given jobs and invaluable to the German Army.

One morning, first thing, my friends and I were loaded onto yet another train, and once again, we were on our way to who-knows-where.[5]

Miracle 5: I was saved by a sandwich, given to me by a German.

During my internment in Flossenbürg, I felt the presence of Moses very strongly. He had made sure I had been given the right job when I was at Mielec, and now that job also carried me all the way through Flossenbürg. Another warm factory, another valued position, and most importantly, extra food. Although my rescuer showed up wearing a German uniform, offering me rare and precious sustenance, I know that it was Moses who was working behind the scenes, ensuring my survival.

During World War II, warplanes were adorned with highly visible emblems.

American fighter planes had the Air Force symbol on their wings: a white star against a black circle sitting on top of a rectangular bar. [Originally, the star was red and there was no rectangle, but too many people mistook the planes for Japanese, so the star was changed to white, and the bar (or "wings") was added to increase overall visibility.]

English fighter planes had a multi-colored bull's-eye on their wings.

German fighter planes had a black square cross, partially outlined in white on the wings, and a black swastika on the tail.

Miracle 6

The Bullets Missed Me

Loaded with the remaining Flossenbürg inmates (those who were still healthy enough to travel), the train slowly pulled away from the concentration camp that had been my unfortunate residence for close to a year. In the mild April air, the cattle-train boxcars had their huge sliding doors wide open. Three German guards sat at the entrance to each, their legs dangling over; their ever-present machine guns held close. I sat on the floor of the car, right in the middle, surrounded by my friends.

We had traveled only about 10 miles down the track, when seemingly out of nowhere, three fighter planes dove into view and pelleted the train with hundreds of bullets. The planes came at us from every direction. We hadn't heard them coming because of the noise from the moving train. I recognized the white star emblem on the underside of the wings that represented the American Air Force. The army that we all hoped would save us one day, was here now, killing us. From the sky, the American pilots could see only the German soldiers lining the doorway entrances along the boxcars. The pilots must have thought they were bombing a German supply train. They didn't realize that the Nazis they saw on the outside were guarding innocent prisoners inside the train.

The exposed German guards were killed first, but the bullets tore right through the wooden slats of the boxcars and also killed many prisoners. I heard the high-pitched zing of metal-on-metal as bullets ricocheted off the train's steel wheels. All of the guards in the car I was in were dead. All of my friends that had been sitting around me were dead. A voice in my head told me to run. In an instant, I burst out from the train, ducking close to the ground and ran under the bullets flying overhead.

I ran a short distance away and lay flat on my belly, watching the horrific events unfolding before me. Smoke bellowed from the locomotive engine where it had exploded into a ball of fire. The engine had been targeted first, stopping the train in its tracks. Almost immediately, the planes came back for a second pass. They dove in at close range and strafed the train again. I could hear the bullets firing and people being hit. Body parts were flying all over the place, and there were many, many killed. Most of the people did not have time to react and were still on the train during that second pass.

Finally, the planes left for good. Maybe the pilots were satisfied that they had taken out the motor, disabling the train, or maybe they realized that some of the people they saw running from the train wore prison stripes. In any case, they never came back.

Once I was sure the planes were gone, I got up from the ground and walked towards the train. Nobody had tried to escape because everything had happened so fast. Besides, there was no place to run to. Though many German guards had been killed, the ones who were left summoned us back and immediately surrounded us.

I stood watching as all of those wounded and dead people were carried out from the train and laid out next to it on the ground; prisoners and soldiers, together. I saw dead bodies missing heads and limbs. I saw people still alive, missing hands, missing legs. They were screaming and crying–it was awful.

The German guards said they were going to call a doctor, but of course, they never did. The guards later told me that those who were injured and couldn't walk were shot dead where they lay. Out of the many thousands of prisoners who had been loaded on the train at Flossenbürg, fewer than 1,000 remained. The guards told us, "We can't go by train anymore, so we will have to walk to the next camp."

And so we walked.

Miracle 6: *The bullets hit just about everything, but missed me.*

Inside the boxcar, I had friends to each side of me–they were killed. I had a friend in back of me–he was killed. The three guards sitting in front of me–they were killed. I was in the middle–I came out without a scratch.

The miracle of my survival can only be explained by the protection and guidance of Moses. And it was Moses who shouted in my ear, "Run!" and saved me from the second round of bullets.

Towards the end of the war, Allied and Soviet forces were closing in on the German Army and the Nazis began to evacuate concentration camps and move the inmates to camps closer to the interior of Germany. They did not want to leave behind witnesses. They were also hoping to keep their slave force working for them.

Many evacuations took place on foot and these came to be known as "Death Marches." Prisoners were forced to walk for miles, day after day, with no food or water provided. The Nazi guards that marched along with them had strict orders to shoot anybody who stopped to rest or could not keep pace.

Many of the marches lasted around two weeks, ending when the Nazis surrendered. An estimated 250,000 concentration camp prisoners were killed or died of exhaustion, exposure, and starvation during death marches.

Miracle 7

Surviving A Death March

We didn't know it at the time, but we had just begun a ten-day "Death March." My friends from the train had all been killed, but over the course of the march, I made new friends. To keep the fighter-plane pilots from spotting us, we avoided the roads and instead walked through the forest by night under cover of the trees. By day, we slept within the woods while German soldiers took turns guarding its mile perimeter to prevent us from escaping.

For 10 days we were given nothing to eat or drink, subsisting only on what we could scrounge. Although the German soldiers had taken supplies from the train, they would not share with us. As we walked through the dark, we grabbed handfuls of anything remotely edible, stuffing our mouths with flowers of the wild blueberry bushes not yet in season. Daylight, however, was our best opportunity to forage. The Nazis guarding the edge of the woods could not see us on the inside, gathering edible mushrooms, flowers, and even grass.

Most of the prisoners became so weakened by the lack of sustenance they simply could not go on. Anyone who fell to the ground had a bullet put through the back of his head, blood spurting out like water from a hose. Of the thousand prisoners who started that walk, only the youngest and strongest 100 finished it.

The planes struck a couple of times during the march. Once again, the pilots saw only the German soldiers stationed on the outskirts of the forest and started shooting, but the powerful fighter-plane bullets went right through the forest towards the prisoners hidden within. The same voice that had told me to run out of the train, told me to take cover. I lay flat on the ground behind a tree alongside my friend, Joseph Korzenik. We could hear the bullets whizzing by above us. It felt like hours that we waited for the planes to fly away before we risked standing up, both of us unharmed. Moses had protected me again.

We covered around 10 miles each night, the Nazis lighting the way with their flashlights. After a couple of nights, we came to the edge of the forest. It opened out onto the fields of a farm where, exhausted and famished, we were able to eat whatever we found growing there. Perhaps we found a source of water–I don't recall as our minds were not clear. I do remember eating celery, which I still enjoy eating to this day, and this provided us with some water as well as sodium. We also ate raw potatoes, carrots, and the first greens we had eaten in years. The raw root vegetables were difficult to bite into in our weakened states, and the greens hurt our stomachs. Nevertheless, we were thankful for every morsel. It was the only night we were able to eat farm vegetables, and the food gave us just enough energy to keep going.

The Nazis herded us into a barn and sent a few of their men to the farmhouse to demand food to replenish the soldiers' supplies. The German family (husband, wife, and another woman, perhaps an adult daughter) was curious about the young men staying in their barn. Given the remoteness of their farm, they had been sheltered from the ravages of war and were frightfully shocked at the sight of us. When the women saw our emaciated, deplorable condition they began to cry. With voices full of sorrow, they said to us, "We didn't know this was going to happen. We didn't know that Hitler was doing this to you." They wanted to bring us food and water, but the soldiers would not let them and sent them away with harsh words. They must have been too afraid to return.

We only slept a couple of hours inside the barn before resuming our march. On we went, walking through the forest at night and sleeping, foraging, or resting four or five hours at a time during the day.

Up to this point, conversation had consisted of the Nazis shouting orders, warnings, and threats. When we first started hearing enemy tanks in the distance, suddenly the captain and his men became less hostile to their prisoners, fearful of the American ground troops that were closing in. The captain told us, "The Americans are just down there. We're getting to the end."

On the afternoon of the 10th day, while resting inside the forest, the captain gathered his 100 remaining prisoners and said, "The Americans are very close. You're going to be liberated soon. We don't want to kill you, but I have orders to shoot you if you try to run. I'm going to give you your lives. You only have to do one thing–do not follow us. We're going to try to escape. You run that way, towards the Americans. You'll be safe. If you follow us, we'll have to kill you."

We were elated. As soon as the German soldiers ran away, we began to walk as fast as our ragged bodies were able in the opposite direction, towards the American troops. In a few miles, we came out of the forest and onto another farm where we saw 35 or 40 American tanks rolling over the fields. The American soldiers saw us coming with our stripes, our wildly waving arms, and our half-dead bodies.

With their tanks surrounding us, the soldiers threw whatever food they had: candy, crackers, even canned goods that we couldn't open. We ate whatever we could without knowing or caring what it was. I started to unwrap something and put it in my mouth, but then realized it was a piece of chewing gum and spit it out.

Throwing food to us was a well-intentioned but misguided effort by the American soldiers to respond to our condition. After going for so long with almost no food, our systems had shut down, and we needed to be very careful about how much and how quickly we ate. Luckily for me, Moses was with me as always, and told me not to eat too much.

The captain of the tank division, who happened to be Jewish, got out of his tank and spoke to us in Yiddish. "Are you Jewish? I am too. We still have a short distance to go to fight the Germans, but we want to bring you to a safe place. I'm going to take you to the next town and make sure those people take care of you until you can get your health back."

We followed behind the tanks on foot, soon arriving at the neighboring town of Cham, Germany (pronounced: Käm), a tiny farm community with one center square surrounded by houses. While the captain's tank was still rolling, he called out for the Bürgermeister (the mayor), who came running over. When the Bürgermeister saw us, he dropped to his knees and implored the captain on behalf of his country, "Please forgive us! We're sorry!" The townspeople came running out of their homes to see what all the commotion was about. The captain told the Bürgermeister, "I'm leaving the survivors of the concentration camp here because they need your help. They need food, clothes, bathing. Take good care of them. Give them anything they need. Remember, I am coming back within a few days. If any of the survivors get hurt, I'm going to kill all of you and burn this whole town down!" He scared them to death. Everyone started running and jumping to do the American's bidding.

The townspeople divided the survivors into groups of about a dozen; each group was sent to a different house, and a nurse was brought in for each house. These kind people gave up their homes, staying overnight in some other place and coming back during the day to help cook, clean, and take care of us. They brought us clean clothes, food, and whatever else they had available. Once inside my assigned house, food and water were the priorities. I felt 75% better after just the tiny amount I was able to eat. Next came a fresh shower and clean clothes. I was no longer a prisoner.

For the first few days, we had very light meals of potato soup, vegetables, and a variety of breads. There was no meat available because it had all gone to the German Army. I watched the townspeople slaughter a young bull in order to better feed us, so within the first week there was plenty of meat.

Our nurse told us how much we could safely eat, and we were all very careful. I ate only a couple of bites at a time. Moses also warned me to take it slowly, making it easier for me to keep control when tempted by a bounty of food such as I had not seen since I was a 13-year-old boy in Kraków.

Sadly, one of the survivors staying at the same house as me ate too much, too fast, and his body went into shock. The nurse desperately tried to pump his stomach to relieve the pressure, but it was too late–he was already gone. The townspeople remembered the words of the American captain. Now that one of us had died, they feared for their own lives when the captain returned.

Each day, I felt a little better. I tried to eat some of every food that was offered, and gradually my stomach returned to normal size. After my full recuperation, there was nothing that I would not eat, even potato soup!

We stayed at Cham until we were well enough to be on our own. During those few months, the people of Cham did everything they could for us; providing clothes, food, and medicine. I never had such good care from Germans.

Miracle 7: I survived a 10-day Death March in which 90% of the people died, and two more times the bullets missed me.

Moses was watching over me–I'm sure of it. I knew what to do because Moses was telling me what to do; to lie flat behind a tree when the planes came, to eat just a little when bombarded with food from the tanks, not to eat too much at once while convalescing. Whatever situation I was in, I had a sense of knowing better than those who didn't make it. Thanks to Moses.

Miracle  8

Finding Family

The American military kept its promise to return to check on the survivors. We were making good progress, so the Americans told us, "Once you are back on your feet, you have to start building a future for yourselves. You can't stay here in this old farm town." The Americans recommended that we go to Frankfurt am Main, Germany, the location of Eisenhower's headquarters and the American Embassy. The prospect of moving on gave us something to think about while we continued to recuperate. There was little to do in Cham, other than sit around the house or walk around the tiny town square. Conversation usually centered around our families–who had survived and who hadn't–and around our futures; what would we do next? Nobody talked about the past. We all knew what had happened and it was best not to focus on it.

> Records show that it was common for the Nazis to list prisoners under a German version of the prisoner's name.
>
> In Arthur's case, his brother Moniek was listed as 'Mendel' and Arthur (Osiek) was (ironically) listed as 'Moses.' According to the Flossenbürg memorial, Moses Neugut arrived with Mendel Neugut in the same crowded train from Plaszow on 8/4/1944 and Mendel died in the Flossenbürg subcamp of Hersbruck on 11/27/1944.

I cannot recall when or from whom I learned that my brother Moniek had died from a lung problem just five months before liberation. I was hardly surprised, and though I was sad, I was mostly numb to the news. After everything I had experienced during almost six years of incarceration, I had become emotionally strong.

Each day at Cham I was becoming physically strong as well, and after three months, I felt well enough to leave. None of us had money, a job, or a home, and few of us had any family left; but the war was finally over, and it was time to move on. Although much of the transportation system had been bombed, and many of the roads were blocked, I decided to take the advice of the Americans and go to Frankfurt am Main. With nothing but the clothes on our backs, my friend Joseph, another fellow, and I began a 200-mile trek on foot. On the way, we took advantage of anything that was moving. We hopped trains that were still running, however short the tracks. We rode buses that came along. We hitched rides with passing trucks and horse-drawn wagons. And we walked.

Along the way, people were kind to us and gave us food and water. All throughout Germany, the citizens were now sympathetic to the plight of the survivors. We had only to show our KL tattoos for people to understand who we were. We slept wherever we could: mostly on the ground. One night, we slept in a train station. Whenever we saw a vehicle, we waved it down and hopped in. Hardly any civilians were traveling through the area, so we hitched rides with American soldiers driving Jeeps with "MP" (Military Police) painted on the sides. It took about two weeks, but eventually, the three of us made it to the big city of Frankfurt am Main.

My first stop was Eisenhower's headquarters. They sent me to the Able Barracks where an American officer typed up a certificate for me to use as official identification. Because the survivors had to be examined before being cleared to find jobs, I was sent across the river to the hospital for a physical. Evidently, the long journey from Cham had taken its toll on me. The doctor felt that I was still not fully recovered, and I was admitted to the hospital where I stayed for 30 days for further treatment and recuperation.

When discharged, I immediately went to a small town just outside of Frankfurt am Main where the American government was providing resources and giving advice to displaced persons. I added my name to the registry for Jewish survivors in case somebody came looking for me. I learned of a job opening at an Officers' Club on the outskirts of Frankfurt am Main and was given information on apartments within walking distance of the Club. I was lucky to find housing because bombing had destroyed so many places. (I bet Moses had a hand in my "good luck.") I signed up for the job at the Officers' Club and was given a few changes of clothes and an American military soldier's uniform to wear to work. I wore the same uniform the GIs wore. It was one of my only possessions.

I worked from the early evenings till about 10 or 11 o'clock at night. I was 19 years old and was very happy to finally be getting paid for my work. After the German concentration camps, I would have been happy with anything. My fellow employees at the Officers' Club were also survivors, most of them Jewish of various nationalities, such as Polish and Russian. There were no Germans at the Club as the American Army had taken over the Club from the German Army and was using it as their base to investigate war criminals.

My job was to make sandwiches and serve beer and liquor. I was also in charge of organizing the evening entertainment for the officers. There was plenty to eat and drink, and I met a lot of people. When you are in a position to provide liquor and sandwiches, you have instant friends! After a couple of drinks, the officers shared all kinds of stories about America. One of the guys was from a big farm near Chicago and would brag, "I have millions of dollars!" America was sounding really good.

After a while, I wanted to go back to the town with the Jewish registry to see if I could find anyone I knew on their list. I flagged down a military Jeep going in that direction. A Jewish-American captain was at the wheel. I climbed in, and he asked me, "Where do you want to go?" I did not understand English, but understood the question and gave him the name of the town. During the ride, he kept talking to me, on and on for 10 minutes. I didn't understand a word. Finally, I showed him my KL tattoo that identified me as a survivor. "Ah!" he said, "Do you speak

> By the end of the war, food and commodities of all sorts were scarce and the German Reichsmark had almost no value. The Allies provided a food ration to the German population but it was too little to live on. As a result, black markets sprang up everywhere in Germany, especially in the cities. Most people risked punishment, including death, to trade goods on the black market just to survive.
>
> Cigarettes became a form of currency. Even many American soldiers got in on the gig. They would trade American cigarettes to Germans for cameras and watches and then send the cameras and watches to the United States to sell for enough money to buy many more cigarettes to trade in Germany.

mameloshn?" (That's Yiddish for "mother language.") I knew just enough Yiddish to get by and was finally able to converse with him a bit. At the registry, I confirmed the death of my brother, but did not find any surviving relatives on the list.

While working at the Officers' Club, I became friends with the mess sergeant in the kitchen. One day, I gave him a bottle of whiskey, and he said to me, "Listen, you can make a lot of money selling coffee on the black market. If you give me liquor, I'll give you the coffee." Right after the war, it was difficult to find products like coffee and cigarettes, so the black market exchange for these items was lucrative. However, he was talking about selling the remains of coffee that had already been brewed. "The Germans won't know the difference!" he assured me. But Moses piped up loudly inside my head, warning me that this was not a good idea. I told the sergeant, "No, thank you." I did not want to get involved with the black market because one day I hoped to go to the United States, and I didn't want to do anything that might prevent that. We stayed friends anyway, and he didn't ask me again.

One captain at the Club was heavily involved with the black market, loading up his Jeep with cartons of cigarettes to sell. He made thousands of dollars, but it was not worth it–he wound up in prison for 20 years. I was extremely glad I had listened to Moses.

After about a year working at the Club, my American officer friends suggested I start thinking about going to the United States. I had picked up the basic English needed for my job: "whiskey," "beer," "sandwich"; but I was nowhere near fluent, and I could not read English at all. Within walking distance of my apartment, there was an older German gentleman offering English lessons, so I signed up for a few nights a week. The officers, seeing my desire to learn, urged me not to waste my time making sandwiches. They advised me that the most important thing I could do was to go to school and get an education. My best friend at the Officers' Club was Sidney Benson, a Jewish-American officer from Syracuse, New York. He agreed with the others: "I know you're having fun now after all you went through, but you'll be better off if you go to the United States and go to school. Don't stay here another day." Though I did not realize it at the time, that was the best advice I got.

I told Sid, "I'm not ready to go anywhere," but my friend was insistent. He even offered to have his family sponsor and take financial responsibility for me, a requirement for getting a Visa to America. Sid convinced me to at least apply.

We went to the American Embassy and signed papers saying Sid was my cousin and that his sister would meet me when I arrived in New York. He had told me about his sister many times, and she and I had written each other. (I even sent her a photograph of myself, but she never sent me her's.) The American government realized that survivors would not have a birth certificate or other form of identification, so the only proof of identity needed was a letter from somebody in the U.S.A. claiming to be a relative. I had that "proof" from Sid's family. I really did have family in America–my Uncle Albert and my aunts, Fannie and Nettie–but I had no idea where they were or how to get in touch with them.

At the Embassy, I told an American consulate that I had been in the concentration camps and was the only survivor from my family in Poland. I showed him the letter from my "pretend family" in America. He asked me if I wanted to go to the United States. I answered, "Of course, but not yet." I was having a good time working at the Officers' Club with all my friends and I didn't want to leave. I had no idea what the United States would be like, and after being isolated from the real world for almost six years, it was hard to imagine a different life.

One week later, Sid told me I was scheduled to go to the United States in two weeks. I gasped, "Already? But that's too fast! I'm not ready to go. I don't even know America." Truthfully, I was a little scared, not knowing the language or anything else about the States.

The American consulate provided me with a Visa, a passport, and all the paperwork I needed to immigrate. The American Embassy would also pay for my transportation, which meant I would not have to use any of the money that I had saved from my job. They even gave me some spending money for when I arrived. I had no more excuses. I was going to America.

I gathered up a small package containing everything I owned in the entire world. I said goodbye to all my American Army buddies, and on a July evening in 1946, just after my 20th birthday, I boarded the SS Marine Perch, headed for my brand new life.

The SS Marine Perch was a Type C4 class ship. These were the largest cargo ships built by the United States Maritime Commission during World War II.

The Marine Perch was converted for carrying troops and made several voyages from Europe back to the United States in 1946.

We left from the major port city of Bremerhaven. The SS Marine Perch was a medium-sized warship filled with sleeping bunks. There were other survivors on the ship, but mostly it was filled with U.S. soldiers. War affairs were wrapping up, and the United States was bringing many of their troops back home.

Inclement weather created massive waves during much of the voyage, and most passengers were motion sick from the violent rocking. Once again, I was lucky. Moses told me to go to the top deck where the air was fresh. Whenever it looked like we were headed for a nasty patch of sea, I ran up top. Even though I didn't feel very well, I never got sick, while the people who stayed below suffered a great deal. It seemed like a very long nine days. It was quite an experience.

Finally, the SS Marine Perch entered the New York harbor. After all the storms I had experienced at sea, the day we made landfall was a nice, clear Saturday afternoon. I could see the Statue of Liberty as the ship pulled into port, but at the time, she didn't mean anything to me; I did not understand that I had just arrived in "the land of the free." My first impression of New York City was that I had never seen so many cars. I commented to the person next to me, "My gosh, there must be a parade!"

So many Europeans had been affected by the war, having no home or family to return to, that in 1945, the United States loosened its restrictions on the number of immigrants allowed into its borders. The Displaced Persons Act of 1948 provided visas to 400,000 immigrants between 1949 and 1952. Of these immigrants, some 68,000 were Jews.

When we arrived, immigrants were given a number to go with a name. Then we waited to be called. When it was my turn, I got off the ship, and Sid's sister (who's name is now lost to me) came to the gate, greeting me with a big smile. We were to spend that night in New York City and then take the morning train to her home in Syracuse. Sid's sister treated me to both lunch and dinner in Manhattan. I was still feeling a bit shaky and unwell from the ocean voyage.

Also, I still had my sea legs, so I wasn't up for much walking; however, I didn't need to go far to be completely bewildered by New York City. Noisy, big, and bustling with activity, I had never seen anything like it. Unlike the Caucasian Eastern Europe I was used to, here there were people of many races and colors. Until I worked at the Officers' Club I'd never seen a black person. Now, I saw black people, white people, and for the first time, Asian people.

Before I arrived, I had little concept of America, although I had attended a meeting on the subject back in Germany and seen pictures of what to expect. The American consulate had shown us photos of the gigantic food markets, taught us how to make a purchase without getting ripped off, and gave us bits of advice such as, "Don't talk to strangers." However, I really could not imagine it until I got there and saw it with my own eyes. I was overwhelmed, but I liked everything I saw. At the same time, I felt off-kilter, facing an unknown future in a strange country where people talk funny. (When I first heard English back in Cham, I remarked to my friend, Joseph, "Americans speak through their noses!" It sounded terrible to me.)

The next morning, Sid's sister and I took an eight-hour train ride, 300 miles north to Syracuse. Syracuse, a small, quiet town with green rolling hills, turned out to be nothing like New York City, even though it is in the same state. My friend, Sid, had left Frankfurt am Main a week before I did, so he was already there when I arrived. His parents and brothers and sisters made a big fuss over me, welcoming me with open arms. They were Jews, originally from Russia, so they spoke Yiddish and Russian, as well as English. They did not speak German or Polish, but between my bits of English and my bits of Yiddish, I was able to manage.

I was in their home only a few days when I figured out why Sid's parents had agreed to sponsor me, and why Sid's sister, rather than Sid, had met me in New York City. Sid's sister must have been close to 30, beyond the age when most girls married in 1946. She and her family were hoping I would develop a romance with her that would lead to marriage, but I was not interested. I was just out of my teens and felt she was much too old for me. Once

I realized what all the fuss was about in Syracuse, New York, I knew I could not stay in that house much longer. I didn't want to hurt his sister's feelings, so I told Sid, "You have a big family and it's too congested for me to live here."

Syracuse was so small that everybody knew everybody else's business. There was a little candy and ice cream store on the corner where all the younger adults gathered. I made several friends right away by hanging out there, and I discussed my awkward situation with them. At that time, most people were very eager to help survivors of the concentration camps, and my new friends were eager to help me, though they didn't ask me much about what I had gone through because they knew it had been very bad. Within two weeks, they found me an apartment nearby, and I moved in using the money I had brought with me from Frankfurt am Main.

Within a week of finding an apartment, I also found a job. Other than serving food, the only type of work I knew was building airplanes, but with the war over, no one needed an airplane mechanic. I walked into a paint store and, in my broken English, asked about employment. Upon learning I had come from the camps, the storeowner wanted to find a way to help me. When he heard that I had worked with aluminum, building planes, he became very excited. Because most of the aluminum in the U.S. had gone to American warplanes, aluminum products were expensive and difficult to find. He got the idea that the store could make good money by offering aluminum storm windows; a specialty product much needed in the northern climate of Syracuse. The owner told me, "If you can build storm windows, you have the job." I said, "Well, let me try."

This job was perfect for me because I didn't have to converse with the public. The boss liked my work very much. I was good at building storm windows, just as I had been good at building planes, and though the smell of hot aluminum reminded me of Mielec and Flossenbürg, I did not let that get to me. I was grateful that I had a job.

I needed more money to support myself living in my own apartment, so after only two weeks, I asked for a raise. My boss said to me, "Osiek, you do such a good job here. If you go to the customers' houses and measure for the storm windows and sell them, you can make a lot more money on commission." I agreed to do that, even though it meant I would be going into people's homes barely able to speak English. As always, I would do my best and try to listen, look, and learn. The only time that my inability to read the language presented a problem was whenever I went to a restaurant; I had no idea what I was ordering!

I had recently written a letter to one of my former neighbors in Kraków, Poland. Because the family was Catholic, not Jewish, I thought they probably still lived there. I used to play with their son who was about my age. They were the ones who always invited me over for Christmas dinner. In the letter, I told them that I had survived the war and was now living in the United States in Syracuse, New York. I gave them my address and phone number in case anybody tried to get in touch with me.

Within a month or two, on a Saturday evening, I was hanging out at the corner store when a friend from my apartment building came running up, shouting, "Osiek! Osiek! You're not going to believe this! You have a telegram from your sister!" My heart leapt. My sister! One of my family members was still alive! Saly had made it safely to the Soviet Union after all. The telegram from Saly read, "I am extremely happy that you survived. I want you to know that we have family in the United States. You have an uncle and two aunts and cousins. Your Uncle Albert lives in Philadelphia." The telegram provided his address. Because Saly had escaped prior to the occupation of Kraków, she had been able to bring some belongings with her, including this information.

About a year after the war, Saly and her husband had left the Soviet Union and returned to our hometown of Kraków to look for family. They had their only child, a daughter, while in Poland. I had been in Frankfurt am Main at that time and had left for America shortly thereafter. Saly visited with all the neighbors we'd been close to, asking if they had heard from anyone. When I sent my letter to Kraków, my former neighbor immediately gave it to Saly who wasted no time sending me the telegram.

After the war, the Soviet Union had occupied Poland. Saly and her family wanted to live in Israel, but the communist government would not let anyone leave the country. When I was in Frankfurt am Main I had also considered returning to Poland to search for family, but the officers at the Club advised me against it. "Do not go to Kraków because they will not let you out," they warned me. "After you arrive, that's it. They'll keep you there."

As soon as I got Saly's telegram, I telephoned the operator for my Uncle Albert's number and called him. When he answered the phone, I told him, "I am your nephew, Osiek Neugut. I'm a survivor from the concentration camps. I've been in the United States just a few months." He knew right away who I was. I had been just a toddler when he had immigrated to America, so I didn't remember him, but he remembered me. "Osiek. Wow!" he exclaimed. He was overjoyed to hear from me. He happened to be having a party at his house that evening and a lot of relatives were there. Uncle Albert shouted to his guests that I was on the phone. Everyone was very happy and excited and they all wanted to talk to me.

One of my cousins got on the phone and said, "My God, you're named 'Osiek'? You're named after my father, do you remember?" I had never heard the story. My mother had an older brother who died long before the war. His Hebrew name was 'Osher.' (That was my Hebrew name too–Osiek is the Polish version.) After Osher died, his children decided to immigrate to America with their Uncle Albert. Before they left, they said to my mother, "If you have another son, name him after our father." I was that son.

The phone was passed around to a few more people, and then my uncle got back on the line and said, "I'm coming to Syracuse to bring you back to Philadelphia. All of your family in the United States is here, and everybody wants to see you." Family. *My* family... At last, I was coming home.

Miracle 8: Finding family in the Land of the Free.

Moses stayed with me even after he saw me safely to liberation. I would not be surprised if he had walked beside me all the way from Cham to Frankfurt am Main and pulled some strings to get me into the Officers' Club. I know for sure that he kept me away from the black market.

Moses Was Watching Over Me

At the Officers' Club, I was blessed to meet a friend like Sid who pushed me to immigrate to America and even gave me the means to do so. Maybe it was Moses who put a rush on my Visa.

Moses saw me through my disagreeable ocean voyage and helped me find a skilled job to support myself in Syracuse. No doubt, he played a role in putting my letter to Kraków in the hands of my only immediate family member still alive, perfectly orchestrating a reunion with the rest of my family.

For America, World War II came on
the heels of the Great Depression. In
Philadelphia it created an industrial boom,
resulting in a population peak in 1945 and
the city's most prosperous era. Philadelphia
helped supply the government's war needs
with ammunition, clothing, tanks, ships,
railroad equipment, and more.

Job opportunities opened up for minorities,
influencing changes in civil rights across the
country. An influx of African-Americans from
the South prompted President Roosevelt
to issue an order in 1941 that prohibited
discrimination when hiring for war-related
work. Many women worked outside
the home for the first time ever in both
traditional gender-role jobs, such as nursing,
and non-traditional jobs, such as welding.

Women also contributed to the war effort by
volunteering to entertain troops and raise
money with war bonds. Public day-care
centers were created during this time and
even though most women returned to the
home at the end of the war, their brief foray
into the working world paved the way for
future equal rights.

As the war drew to a close, many of
the jobs created by it were no longer
needed. Workers were laid off and a lot of
businesses closed. But the civil rights issues
raised by the labor needs of the war were
brought to light and provided the stepping-
stones to future change.

Miracle 9

A Family Of My Own

My uncle Albert dropped everything and took the train to Syracuse that very night to bring me back to Philadelphia. The paint store had plans for me to start the following day working on commission selling the storm windows, but my plans had now changed. Family was more important. I told my friends to explain my disappearance to my boss, and I left Syracuse behind.

My Aunt Nettie and her husband offered me their extra room. They lived on top of their grocery store in Southwest Philadelphia near 69th Street, which in those days was a very nice area. Once again, I had to adjust to my new surroundings. Philadelphia was a very large city and quite a change from Syracuse, but it was where my family lived, so it was where I belonged.

My first six months there were good times. As I was not yet working, I spent the days getting used to my new life and getting acquainted with my "new" family. Everybody wanted to meet me and show me around. Aunt Fannie invited me to Brooklyn where she lived with her daughter. Lillian, a first cousin from Elizabeth, New Jersey, invited me to stay at her beach house. Eventually, I met all of my relatives who had been at Uncle Albert's party the day I first called him.

I was also reunited with my cousin Max, who had escaped the war via the underground and was now living in New York City. All around the U.S.A. and Europe, people who had lost touch during the war were finding each other again. Somebody would put an ad in a newspaper like The New York Times or Jewish Exponent, and contact information was passed around until it reached the right person.

My army officer friend from Chicago wrote and told me that my fellow survivor Joseph Korzenik was living in New Haven, Connecticut with his uncle. I called Joe, and he invited me to visit. Joe and I stayed in touch for 20 or 30 years after the war. Because we had been through such terrible times together, we felt comfortable advising each other on all aspects of our lives. But we never talked about what had happened to us. The only comment Joe made about the war was, "Do you remember when you and I were hiding behind that tree and the bullets were flying all around us? That was something!"

I also stayed in touch with Sid. While living in Syracuse, I had started dating Sid's first cousin. She and I continued to date for a little while after I moved to Philadelphia. We would each take the train to New York City to split the distance between us.

> Even before the end of the war, Jewish people worldwide planned to demand financial compensation from Germany for the Nazi's crimes against them.
>
> In Israel, the issue was divided. Many Jews felt that to accept German money was an insult to all they had suffered, but the Israeli government argued that it would take money to help their Jewish immigrants and Germany should be held responsible.
>
> Since reparations began, Germany has paid billions of dollars to Holocaust victims the world over.

After I had visited with all my friends and relatives, I went to an office in Philadelphia to apply for reparations for survivors. I had a better chance of getting a higher pension if a psychiatrist confirmed that I really did experience that trauma. I did everything required to ensure I got the maximum benefit. The doctor heard my story and told me, "It is amazing that you survived; you deserve everything the law allows."

I told the doctor about the recurring nightmares I was having. Nazi guards were chasing me with their machine guns, and I was running as fast as I could, flying through grassy fields, until I ran right over the edge of a cliff. Just as I felt my feet leave the ground, I would jerk awake, my heart pounding. I thought it strange to be having nightmares then. I never had any during the actual war.

The psychiatrist explained to me that while I had been in the camps under such extreme stress, I had been in survival mode and could not reflect upon my situation. Once I was safe and able to relax, my mind started to think about all that had happened to me, and I was finally experiencing the effects of what I went through. I continued to have nightmares for two years. Reflecting on my past, I could not understand how people could treat other people so badly, and I could not figure out why God would let so many people die for nothing.

The pension I received from the German government included reparations for the murder of my parents, for the years I had worked in the camps without pay, and for the loss of my education. The money was enough as long as I was living rent-free with my aunt, but that situation did not last long. Aunt Nettie seemed to have a lot of little complaints about me, and one of her neighbors complained to her that I undressed in front of the window. I wasn't happy with Aunt Nettie's ways either. She always left lint on the glasses after drying them. One day, she saw me rinsing her "clean" glasses before drinking from them and asked, "Don't you trust my washing?" That's when I knew it was time to leave.

I knew that to get ahead I needed an education. My family could not support me while I went to school, so I had to find a job. Though I asked around everywhere, there were no airplane factories in the area to work for. The warplanes were being dismantled and the commercial airline industry had not yet reached Philadelphia.

A cousin suggested I apply for work at a cabinet-making company. With my new job and my pension, I was able to move to an apartment in Wynnefield on 54th Street, near City Line Avenue, a well-known area with a large population of wealthy Jews. Typical of the times, the apartment came already furnished, so I didn't have to buy anything new, and it was easy to move what few possessions I had acquired.

To pass the United States citizenship test, immigrants must correctly answer six out of 10 questions chosen from a list of 100 by a naturalization examiner. The questions are facts about America's history, geography, and government, such as "Why does the flag have 13 stripes?"

Over time the citizenship test has become more and more standardized. This has resulted in a test that is fair and efficient, but in many ways is nothing more than a test of memorization rather than a true understanding of one's new country.

Once again I was fortunate that the owner of the company where I worked recognized my potential. He said to me, "You know, you should be learning something more than this." So I decided to take night classes at Bartram High School to become a U.S. citizen.

I worked during the day and went to school from 7 to 10 PM, learning English and American history. Because I was well spoken in English and a fast learner, the teacher selected me as his number-one student. At the graduation ceremony, he asked me to give a speech in front of everybody. "Just go out there and tell them you've only been here in the United States a short time, and tell them what you've accomplished," he said. I was not expecting this, so I was completely unprepared. When I got up to the podium, I saw all those eyes staring at me and I froze. Knowing that my teacher was waiting expectantly behind me, pulled me out of my daze. I gave a short speech and everybody clapped. Afterward, I was glad for the experience.

After graduation, I studied for the citizenship test, passed, was sworn in with a group of other immigrants, and got my naturalization papers[6]. Back when I was working at the Officer's Club in Frankfurt am Main, I had already felt like an American—now it was official!

At that time, I also changed my name from 'Osiek Neugut' to 'Arthur Neigut.' I wanted my last name to match Uncle Albert's. He had changed the spelling to 'Neigut' when he immigrated so that it would be easier for Americans to pronounce correctly. I changed my first name to 'Arthur' because my Hebrew first name is 'Osher' and 'Arthur' is the closest American equivalent.

At work, my boss wanted me to observe what was going on in the shop rather than do any physical work. He told me, "I want you to learn how to run the business, not just nail cabinets together." He was a kind and interesting person and would give me money to go to a restaurant and buy myself lunch, telling me, "Sit as long as you like. Don't rush back."

I worked at the cabinet company while continuing to go to night school. Now that I was a U.S. citizen, I was able to enroll in a high school for free. For the first year, I went to Dobbins vocational high school. Sometimes I overheard my fellow students talking about me, wondering where I was from. Was I French? German? My accent had become a mix of so many different languages. Since I was working with cabinetry, I choose the closest field of study at Dobbins: manufacturing furniture. In addition to regular high school subjects like math and reading, I learned how to design furniture and read blueprints. I graduated with the equivalent of a high school diploma.

Moses Was Watching Over Me

I knew I wanted to create materials within a business environment, so after graduating Dobbins, I went to business school at a private college in Levittown and then to Temple University for technical school to learn architecture. I was not concerned about getting a diploma. I only took courses that were interesting or practical, but not all the courses that were required, so I did not graduate from either school. The same good eye for detail that had served me so well in the airplane factories, proved to be an advantage in drawing blueprints.

It was not easy working all day long and then going to school until 10 at night. Sometimes, I would doze off at my desk. My Temple professor said to me, "Don't you fall asleep, Arthur. You have too much talent." That gave me the motivation to continue. I spent many, many nights at school.

When the cabinet company went out of business, my boss recommended that I go work for The Ross Company. They were located at Front and Walnut Streets and manufactured furniture for restaurants. He knew the owner, Harry Ross, and put in a good word for me. When I went to interview with Harry and his wife, Mae, they had already heard about me. They knew I was a good worker and had studied their line of business, so they hired me immediately.

Working for the Rosses marked the beginning of a long, successful career, as well as the beginning of the most important part of my life. Every day, I rode the same bus to and from work with the bookkeeper, Vivienne, so we became friends. Vivienne was engaged to be married, and she invited me to her wedding. That's where I first met Thelma Ross, the boss's daughter.

Vivienne had a feeling that Thelma and I would get along, so she made sure to seat us next to each other at the wedding. Even Thelma's mother, Mae, had said to Thelma, "Wait 'til you meet him–he's got blue eyes!" Thelma looked very beautiful in her dress, and as we talked, I could tell that she was an extraordinarily kind person. I asked her to dance and then asked if I could see her again. We dated for two years, but I knew almost from the start that I wanted to marry her. Her sweet disposition was what I loved most about her.

When I started dating Thelma, the Rosses frequently invited me to their house for dinner. Thelma knew that I had been in the concentration camps, but she never asked me about it. The whole subject was upsetting to her, so she never wanted to hear any details. Still, I could feel her empathy; she had been through her own pain and suffering, having had asthma her whole life.

When I asked Harry's permission to marry his daughter, he agreed, and Thelma and I began to plan our future. I had no idea what I was going to do about a ring. As luck would have it, Mae's father owned a jewelry store, so Mae offered to take Thelma and me there. Thelma picked out a lovely (and expensive) engagement ring. The only thing left to do was for me to officially ask Thelma for her hand in marriage.

One evening, Thelma and I were enjoying dinner at a kosher restaurant at 4th and Arch Streets. The place was so narrow, the waiter kept bumping into me as he passed by carrying dishes. Though I had nothing preplanned, I asked Thelma to marry me during that dinner, and of course, she said, "Yes!" Thelma and I were married on January 20th, 1952.

Thelma was working at Abington Hospital as a laboratory technician (phlebotomist). True to her nature, she had a particularly gentle touch, and the youngest, most fragile patients were sent her way. I continued to work at The Ross Company, rising up through the ranks, eventually becoming president in charge of 35 employees. I designed the plans and built and manufactured the furniture for bars, restaurants, banks, and more. Who could have imagined that I would go from being a Polish immigrant with an 8th grade education, to running a successful business in America?

I had not seen my Uncle Albert for quite a while. One day, he came to The Ross Company to meet me for lunch. Just two weeks later, he died at age 93.

I wrote letters to my brother Itzhak. When one of my foremen at The Ross Company traveled to Argentina, I gave him Itzhak's address and he visited with him. The foreman told me that Itzhak looked a lot like me and had two sons who worked as policemen. Since I was still a baby when Itzhak went to Argentina, I did not remember anything about him, but Itzhak remembered that right before he left Poland, he had held me in his arms to say goodbye. I never did get to see him before he died.

During my years in Philadelphia, I kept in touch with my sister Saly and her family. We wrote letters back and forth and I sent her care packages. I was doing well in America, and she was having a tough time still confined to communist-controlled Poland, so I tried to help out as much as possible. I sent her money, clothing, tea, coffee, and other essentials until she and her family were able to leave Poland and immigrate to Israel. I did not actually see

Saly again until 23 years later, when I flew to Israel to attend the wedding of her daughter, Miriam. It was an emotional reunion.

On March 28th, 1957, Thelma and I were thrilled at the birth of our first-born, a boy we named Kenneth, and doubly so when the hospital where Thelma worked announced his birth over their loudspeaker system. Thelma quit her job of 15 years to take care of Kenny and never went back to work. Three years later, on September 1st, 1961, our daughter, Susan, was born.

Since I was now an American, I thought it fitting to introduce my son to the great American pastime of baseball, but Kenny never really took to it. Rather, I was the one who became an avid Phillies fan. I still watch the games whenever I can. When Kenny was still a little boy, I taught him Polish. It wasn't long before he was speaking nothing but Polish, and I had to stop the lessons because Thelma complained that she could not understand her son. Kenny seemed to have a knack for languages, so when he began studying German in high school he quickly became fluent and won many German language awards.

I always advised my children that the most important thing in life is to have an education. Kenny took that to heart, spending many nights studying in his room behind a closed door. He was a straight-A student and skipped grades in high school and college. He was one of only two students to be accepted into Hahnemann University medical school while still a junior in high school, and he went on to become a radiologist.

Susie looks a lot like my sister Erna Esther with her large eyes and black hair. She was a playful child and liked to shadow me in the garden as I tended to our peach, plum, and pear trees, and to our blueberry bush. Our neighbors baked pies for us with the shopping bags full of fruit Susie and I gave them.

Susie went to Philadelphia College of Art. She became a pearl-stringer and worked for many years on Jewelers' Row in center city Philadelphia. Over the years, she made beautiful pieces of jewelry to give to her mother. Now she is a full-time mom herself and part-time pharmacy technician. These days, she enjoys tending her own garden and still creates jewelry to give as gifts. I think she gets her artistic talent from me.

Our family spent many wonderful years together. We always enjoyed a beautiful Thanksgiving dinner. Thelma and I were a great team as she made the stuffing and the side dishes, and I cooked the turkey, basting it every half hour, and then carving it. Thelma sat down every day to the grand piano in our living room, filling our home with classical music. She played so beautifully, the neighbors would stand outside of our house just to listen. Every summer for many years, we spent a week or two in Margate at the New Jersey shore. We enjoyed numerous other family vacations as well, traveling to Florida, New England, Canada, and the Pocono mountains. I was always the official driver. When I drove in heavy snow that kept most people indoors, Susie remarked that my concentration camp days made me fearless. She's right. I have a unique outlook on life. I've seen the worst, so not much easily fazes me. Ironically, the Holocaust made me into a perpetual optimist.

Miracle 9: Starting a family of my own.

I don't believe it was coincidence that I started working for Harry and Mae Ross. I believe Moses set it up that way, knowing that Thelma was the one for me. Hitler may have tried to wipe the Jews off the face of the earth, but Moses intervened, and now the Neigut family lineage continues. Ken blessed me with two granddaughters: Jessica (who now has a son of her own) and Rebecca; and Susie blessed me with two grandsons: Andrew and Daniel. I am very proud of my children and their children.

Miracle 10

A New Lease On Life

On July 2, 2006 my beloved Thelma, my wife of 54 years, passed away. As soon as I heard from the hospital, I called each of my children. Susie was in Margate with her husband and sons. I told her, "Your mother went up to Heaven." Strangely enough, just seconds prior to my call, Susie's youngest son, Daniel (who was celebrating his seventh birthday), had looked up at the ceiling and from out of the blue declared, "Someday, I'm going to be in Heaven."

Thelma's health had deteriorated considerably in the last 10 years of her life. Having suffered from asthma since childhood, she developed Chronic Obstructive Pulmonary Disease and had severe spine-deforming osteoporosis, both of which interfered with the function of her lungs. She became increasingly frail and struggled to breathe on a daily basis. It was a difficult time, but I was dedicated to her throughout her illness. Many times during those years, she was unable to function and relied on me to feed, bathe, and dress her. Depression had set in. She would not eat or drink and refused to take any medications. The doctors told me "there is nothing we can do." She spent a lot of time in and out of Abington Hospital, the same place where she had been working when we first met.

Despite her illness, Thelma continued to play her piano every day. She even played for the nurses and other patients one time while in the hospital. The only other thing that she still seemed to enjoy was going to the casinos in Atlantic City, New Jersey to play the slots, so I took her there once a week. Thelma seemed to have a knack for winning at gambling. One time, Thelma and I were walking through the Hilton casino and something was telling me to play the machine in front of us. I looked at Thelma and said, "I'm going to put $3 in that machine." We won $1,000. Another time, Thelma played number 4949 in the Pennsylvania lottery. The man in line behind her said, "Lady, that's some number you're playing!" The numbers came out in the exact order she played them: 4-9-4-9, and she won $2,900.

Moses may have been with us at the casinos and lottery, but during the times that Thelma was sick, I could not feel his presence as I had felt it in the camps. I was simply too heartbroken.

I had stopped working at The Ross Company with the intention of retiring, but with Thelma so ill, I needed the money as well as some time away from such a sad situation.

There was a company called Trenton China in center city Philadelphia that sold restaurant equipment. I was friendly with the owner, Sam Adelson, as he had patronized The Ross Company over the years. I called Sam up and said, "I'm stuck at home and I need something to do, so I would like you to give me a job." He was concerned that he had no office for me or other amenities for a man in my previous position, but he said, "Come in. You have a job–whatever you want to do."

I started out working for him two days a week as a salesperson. He said, "Arthur, you do such a terrific job, how about working four days?" Since The Ross Company and Trenton China had many customers in common, I already knew a lot of the folks who stopped in and that made the work even more enjoyable. The customers began asking for me, and soon I was working five days a week.

Trenton China was a treasure for serious cooks. It carried every type of pot, pan, dish, and cooking implement, and I quickly learned the whole inventory–I could tell you what every item in that store was used for and its price. When customers who were looking to open a new restaurant came into the store, not only could I help them choose all of the supplies they would need, but I could also draw them a detailed floor plan. When I ate out at restaurants, I knew the name and number of every pattern of dish put in front of me. Sam and I went out to lunch often. A lot of our meals were free because the restaurant owners knew us. Sam's wife would call him to bring her back some food and she always asked for me. She would jokingly say, "Let me talk to my boyfriend."

I worked Monday through Friday until I was 80 years old. Susie and I carpooled together, leaving the house at 6 AM to drive to center city where she would go to Jewelers' Row and I to Trenton China. After work, if Thelma was in the hospital, I would visit her every day. It tore me up to see her lying in that hospital bed. She would reach her arms out to me and with her small voice say, "Arthur!" The nurses were witness to this heart-wrenching scene.

When Thelma died, Trenton China gave me two weeks off with pay, and my neighbors got together and gave me a gift certificate to the nearby Tiffany Diner. I asked them, "What is this for?" and they said it was because I took such good care of Thelma. Now, they told me, it's time for me to relax and go out to eat. Once, I tried to cook for myself, but when I looked at what I had made, I said, "Forget it." Instead, I took to eating lunch at the diner with a group of male friends almost every day and went out every night for dinner with whomever was available. I talked to Susie on the phone daily and treated her and her sons to lunch every Wednesday. Susie was a great help to me, keeping me company and also cleaning my house for me until I found a cleaning lady.

For the first six months after Thelma's death, I seemed to be on a winning streak with the lottery. I felt that Thelma was looking down on me from Heaven, giving me the winning numbers. Six times in four weeks I won! One time I took some shirts to my cleaner and he convinced me to play the lotto. I played 358 (part of my car license) and I won $1,000. I went by myself to the Hilton casino and played a little bit here and there, but I kept losing. Then I played one of the machines that Thelma used to play. I put $3 in and with the first try I won $1,350! I thought, "Wow!" and decided to call it a day.

I continued to work at Trenton China for about a year after Thelma's death. Then I went into the hospital for intestinal surgery. Since early in my marriage, I had suffered from Crohn's disease. I suspect it is the result of never speaking about what had happened to me in the war. For so many years, I held all of that inside and it rotted away at me. After my surgery, I never went back to work.

My life had changed dramatically. Thelma was gone, my children were grown with families of their own, and now I had no job to occupy me. Though I could still feel Thelma's presence in the house and I tried to keep busy, I was very lonely.

All the waitresses who worked at the Tiffany Diner knew I was a widower and everyone wanted to set me up with somebody. I went on about half a dozen first dates that never led to a second and for two years I was alone.

One day, Susie's mother-in-law had a party with extended family. Susie called to invite me. "They'll have dinner there," she said. "Instead of sitting by yourself at home, come with us." I was glad I went because it was at that party where I first met Joyce.

Joyce's sister had been wanting Joyce to meet me for a while, thinking we would be a good match. After all, within Joyce's age group, I was considered a "catch" because I still had most of my hair and could drive at night. Joyce wasn't so anxious. She was a widow of six years, and though she was also lonely, was not really looking to meet anybody.

I was sitting on a bench by myself at the party when Joyce sat down at the other end. Little by little, she started moving towards me and I started moving towards her. It was summertime and I was wearing short sleeves. She asked me about my KL tattoo. I told her that I had been in the concentration camps, but never talk about it and she did not press me further. I found out that she is a Conservative Jew and keeps kosher, lives in Princeton New Jersey (about a 45-minute drive away), is a retired physician at Princeton University, and at 71, she is 12 years younger than I. Though I enjoyed talking with her, neither of us thought much of that initial meeting.

It wasn't until a month later on the fourth of July that I asked Susie, "Do you think it's alright if I call Joyce for a date? I don't think she knows how old I am." Susie confirmed for me that Joyce would be interested if I called her, and a week or two later, I found the courage to ask Joyce on a dinner date. When Joyce arrived at the restaurant, I was standing out front waiting for her with a big smile on my face. We enjoyed our dinner, and to tell the truth, I was smitten. I invited her back to see my house and watch the Phillies ballgame. Susie called during the game to find out how my first date went. "She's still here," I told Susie. I think Susie was surprised!

Right away, Joyce and I had a very good relationship and we quickly became a couple. I started regularly attending synagogue with Joyce, despite a general reluctance towards religion since childhood. (With Thelma, I had gone only on holidays as a way to pay my respects to Moses for having saved me.) And although Joyce keeps kosher, I am still not interested. For the rest of the summer of 2008, we saw each other sporadically, as Joyce did a lot of traveling. In December, I went into the hospital for knee replacement surgery and from there, was sent into a rehabilitation facility for eight weeks. Joyce visited me each week and we grew closer. Once I was out of rehabilitation, I wanted to be with Joyce all the time. One day, I blurted out, "Is it okay if I tell people we're engaged?"

Joyce replied, "Arthur, we hardly know each other! Besides, you haven't asked me to marry you yet. You need to ask me to marry you, and you need to give me a ring or something that says we're engaged." We went to a jewelry store to pick out a diamond and emerald ring and were officially engaged in the spring of 2009 with plans for a summer wedding.

My daughter was happy for me that I was no longer alone, but she also struggled with the idea of me remarrying because she felt it was a betrayal to her mother. Susie told me that the night before the wedding, Thelma came to her in a dream and said, "It's okay–I'm happy for him. He needs somebody."

Joyce and I celebrated with an aufruf at Joyce's synagogue, the Princeton Jewish Center. All three of Joyce's sons were there to read from the Torah. The next day, Sunday, August 16, 2009, we

The aufruf (Yiddish for "calling up") is the first public announcement of an upcoming Jewish wedding. In this tradition, held the Shabbos before their wedding, the bride and groom are called to the Torah and the Rabbi makes a blessing over them.

At the conclusion, the congregation may throw nuts, raisins, and candy at the couple to bless them with a sweet and fertile marriage.

In a traditional Jewish wedding, the couple is married under a canopy called a chuppah (pronounced hoopa or koopa). The chuppah symbolizes the couple's new home and is open on all four sides to symbolize the hospitality of welcoming people to their home, just as Abraham and Sarah welcomed people to their open tent.

were married by the Rabbi at the synagogue under a chuppah. Joyce's son, David, who had flown in from Israel, walked Joyce down the aisle. Joyce's 96-year-old mother was there as well, along with my daughter, Susie, her husband, Jeff, and their two children. Susie walked me down the aisle.

Once we were married, Joyce and I did a lot of traveling. It seemed like we were constantly on the go. On several occasions, we stayed at both of Joyce's timeshares, one of them in the Berkshire Mountains in Massachusetts and the other in Orlando, Florida. While in Florida, we were able to visit Joyce's brother and my son, Kenny, and his wife. Kenny had not come to the wedding, so it was nice to see him after such a long time. He took us out to dinner and we had fun at his house watching T.V. on his movie-projector-sized screen. We visited with each of Joyce's three children, one in New York City, one in Maryland, and one in Israel.

While in Israel, Joyce and I enjoyed dinner in Tel Aviv with my niece, Miriam, and her husband, Reuven. My sister Saly had passed away several years earlier. Joyce commented during dinner, "Fifty years later, enjoying one another's company; this contradicts everything Hitler tried to do. We are living proof he did not achieve his goal. The ultimate rebuttal!"

Joyce encourages and supports me talking about my concentration camp days, something I had never wanted to do in the past. Her daughter-in-law, Sarah, is Director of Admissions at a school in New York City. During the school's Holocaust program, Sarah asked me to speak to a class of 13-year-olds about my experience. I was a little nervous at the idea, but felt better knowing that Joyce would be there with me. I felt it was something that the kids should know about and hear first-hand from a living survivor. The children sat around me in a circle and listened to my story. Later, the class sent me a thank you card. It was a good feeling.

Miracle 10: Moses gave me a new lease on life.

After losing Thelma, I believe Moses saw to it that I would not spend the rest of my days alone. Getting remarried at 83 years old is a miracle in and of itself. I'm truly blessed that Moses guided me to meet Joyce. Susie likes to joke, "Not bad, Dad–a Jewish doctor!" Together, Joyce and I have been on many adventures and met many wonderful people. Though I lost most of my family in the war, these days, I feel like my family just keeps growing. I drew a picture of a duck for Joyce's 4-year-old grandson, Coby. Since then, he always asks Joyce, "When is Arthur coming? I love Arthur." He is unbelievable. And I am so blessed.

It is now 68 years after the end of World War II. Those who were children during the war are now in their 70s and 80s. It is estimated that less than 130,000 survivors are still living in the United States. It is impossible to know for sure, as many chose to never reveal their survivor status.

While we are moving towards a time when there will no longer be eyewitnesses to the Nazi regime, there are many institutes, museums, scholars, and other individuals and groups who work to preserve the history of the Holocaust and the memories of those who lived it.

Epilogue

I am now 87 years old. My walking is a bit slow, and I take the stairs carefully. No question about it: I am an "old man." And yet, so many survivors who went through the horrors I did either never made it to this age, or they left the camps emotionally crippled. I may be aging, but I still feel healthy, strong, and happy. My doctor says I have the body of a much younger man. He tells me, "At the rate you're going, you will live to be 105!"

Most would agree that I would be justified to be bitter and angry over what happened to my family and me. Though I did suffer emotionally and physically, if anything, I am even happier for it because I take nothing good for granted. There isn't much I worry about and I'm very good at putting things in perspective. I'd rather joke and make others feel good than sit and complain. My daughter tells the story of my reaction after serious intestinal surgery in which I had several feet of colon removed. I was in the recovery room and the nurse let Susie bring me my glasses. All the patients were moaning in pain and looking miserable, but I was smiling and waving to her! She thinks that's hilarious...and typical of me.

People ask me why I never belonged to one of the many organizations available to survivors. For many years, I was certainly too busy going to night school, but more importantly, I could never talk about it. When I was with Thelma, she never wanted to hear about it because it was so upsetting to her. I did not tell my kids either because I didn't want them to be upset.

The first time I really spoke about my experience during the war was when I agreed to participate in the Shoah Foundation project initiated by Steven Spielberg. It was not easy for me. I had been up the whole night before the interview, sick to my stomach from nerves. If you watch the tape, you can see that I almost never smile until I mention my family, and that I am going to have my first grandson, Andrew.

Years later, my son, Kenny, finally sat down to watch that interview. He said, "I never knew everything you went through to survive, especially being on that train overnight in front of Auschwitz. It's amazing to me because you never discussed this with us, so I didn't have any interest in it until my wife and I watched the Shoah tape. It's a miracle!" Now he is interested. Now he wants to know.

And now, I want to express all of the things I went through.

The more I think about it, I cannot believe that the whole world let this happen. As a young man I did not fully understand, and I still ask the question, "Why did this happen?"

Though I have no desire to ever go back to Germany, I have nothing against the German people. I went to school with a lot of Germans and they were very nice people. I believe that all of the Nazis and all those who participated in carrying out the crimes of the Holocaust are probably dead now anyway.

Each step along the way of my life has been a miracle orchestrated by Moses. The sheer reality of surviving the camps, finding my relatives after the war, marrying Thelma and raising a family, building a career, marrying Joyce and expanding my family–these are all miracles to me. But the true miracle of my life is my positive attitude. You cannot look back with regret and say, "maybe this, maybe that." You have to do the best you can. Make the most of what life gives you, and smile.

To hear Arthur Neigut's voice, go to www.MosesWasWatchingOverMe.com for free audio clips from his original interviews.

Timeline Of Events

Date	Event	Arthur's Age
June 13, 1926	Arthur/Osiek is born	Birth
September 1, 1939	Nazis invade Poland	13 y.o. and in 8th grade
Within the first two weeks of September 1939	Nazis occupy Arthur's street	13 y.o.
Autumn of 1939 (Arthur guesses that occupation lasted a few weeks to one month)	Taken to Ghetto in Poland	13 y.o.
Probably October 1939 (Within a week of entering Ghetto)	Sent to labor camp in Poland	13 y.o.
Late 1939/early 1940 (A couple of months into being at the labor camp)	Liquidation of ghetto	13 y.o.
During 1940 or 1941 (Arthur guesses he was at the labor camp for six months to one year)	Transported to Mielec, Poland	14 or 15 y.o.
May 1944	Mielec evacuated because Russian Army is near	17 y.o.
May 1944	Train stop at Auschwitz, Poland	17 y.o.

Date	Event	Arthur's Age
May 1944 to August 4, 1944	Intermediate camps before arriving at Flossenbürg: Poland and Germany	17–18 y.o.
August 4, 1944	Transported to Flossenbürg, Germany	18 y.o.
November 27, 1944	Brother Moniek died in the Flossenbürg sub-camp of Hersbruck, Germany	Arthur is 18 y.o. (Two days before this day, Moniek would have turned 21 y.o.)
April 14 or 15, 1945	Flossenbürg is evacuated/train is strafed	18 y.o.
April 14 or 15–23, 1945	10-day death march in Germany	18 y.o.
April 23, 1945	Liberation, Bavaria, Germany	18 y.o.
April 23, 1945 to middle of summer (Arthur thinks it was about three months)	Convalescing in Cham, Germany	18–probably 19 y.o.
Summer 1945 (took about two weeks)	Walk to Frankfurt am Main, Germany	Probably 19 y.o.
Summer 1945	30-day recuperation in Frankfurt am Main hospital	Probably 19 y.o.
Late Summer/early Autumn 1945	Working at Officer's Club (Frankfurt am Main, Germany)	19 y.o.

Date	Event	Arthur's Age
June 1946	Nine-day voyage on SS Marine Perch, arriving in New York harbor, U.S.A.	20 y.o.
June 1946 to Winter 1947 (He thinks he was there about six months)	Living in Syracuse, New York, U.S.A.	20 y.o.
Winter 1947	Move to Philadelphia, Pennsylvania, U.S.A.	20 y.o.
Around 1949 or 1950 (He met Thelma here and dated her for two years before marrying her)	Working at The Ross Company, Philadelphia, Pennsylvania, U.S.A.	Probably began at 22 y.o.
January 20, 1952	Marries Thelma	25 y.o.
March 11, 1952	Became a U.S. citizen	25 y.o.
March 28, 1957	Kenny is born	30 y.o.
September 1, 1961	Susie is born	35 y.o.
August 1996	Interview with the Shoah Foundation	70 y.o.
1996–2006	Working at Trenton China	From 70–80 y.o.
July 2, 2006	Thelma dies	80 y.o.
August 16, 2009 (They met summer 2008)	Marries Joyce	83 y.o.

Neigut Family Tree

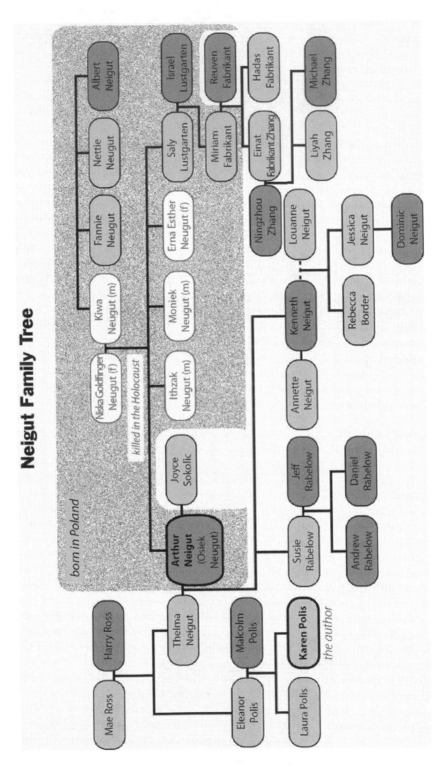

born in Poland

killed in the Holocaust

the author

The only photograph Arthur has of himself as a child (given to him after the war by his Uncle Albert).

Arthur is sitting on the stool in the middle (about one year old). Standing behind him are his mother, Niska and his father, Kiwa. Sitting next to Kiwa is Arthur's paternal grandfather, and next to him is Arthur's Uncle Albert. Standing next to Niska is one of Arthur's aunts (either Fannie or Nettie). Sitting in front of Niska is Arthur's paternal grandmother, and she is holding the hand of his brother Moniek.

Arthur and Thelma's Wedding
January 20, 1952

Arthur preparing to walk down the isle

Thelma with her parents, Harry and Mae Ross,
preparing to walk down the isle

Arthur and Thelma Neigut, newly married
and standing beneath the chuppah

Uncle Albert and his wife
walk Arthur down the isle

Thelma and Arthur with
baby Kenny, 1957

At the shore with
baby Kenny

Arthur with
Kenny and
Susie. Harry
Ross sits in the
background,
1962

Moses Was Watching Over Me

Arthur tending his
peach trees with Kenny
(9 y.o.), 1966

Arthur's business card and Arthur in his office, 1969

Arthur with his sister
Saly and her husband,
Israel at the wedding of
Saly and Israel's daughter,
Miriam, 1970

Arthur with his
niece, Miriam,
on her wedding
day, 1970

Ken, Thelma,
Arthur, and Susie
at Ken's graduation
from medical
school, 1982

Arthur with granddaughter
Jessica, 1984

Susie and Jeff Rabelow,
married May 15, 1991

Arthur and Joyce
with Ken and his wife,
Annette at Andrew
Rabelow's Bar
Mitzvah, 2009

Arthur and Joyce's Wedding
August 16, 2009

Holding up the Ketubah (Hebrew marriage agreement)

With Joyce's 96-year-old mother, Frances (known as "Granny Franny")

Moses Was Watching Over Me

Andrew Rabelow's Bar Mitzvah
November 21, 2009

Susie and Jeff with their sons, Andrew and Daniel.
Andrew is wearing a tallis and holding a prayer book.

Susie sits with her sons, Andrew and Daniel.
Behind her are Jeff, Joyce, and Arthur.

Endnotes

1   This is Arthur Neigut's experience, as he remembers it. I have tried to verify facts wherever possible or add endnotes where I noticed discrepancies between Arthur's account and other historical resources. For the most part, I left Arthur's words and/or their meaning intact to capture his unique perspective on *his* story.

2   Arthur remembers the name "Zakliczyn" as the ghetto he went to; however, historical reference of the timeframe Zakliczyn was established and the deportation route it used are inconsistent with Arthur's memory of these aspects. It is most likely that he was sent to a different ghetto within Poland.

3   Arthur does not know exactly when he received the KL tattoo, but according to another survivor's story (http://www.megdal.com/Meyer/Testimony.htm), these tattoos were given just prior to evacuation of Mielec.

4   Arthur is not positive whether or not he had socks at Flossenbürg. Resources indicate that socks were a luxury in the camps. Since Arthur was among the "elite" group of airplane mechanic prisoners, he may have had this luxury.

5   Flossenbürg concentration camp evacuated its prisoners south towards the camp of Dachau.

6   The way that Arthur tells his story, he became a U.S. citizen before he met Thelma Ross. However, his naturalization papers state the date as 3/11/52, which is after he married Thelma.

Sidebar References

Introduction
http://sfi.usc.edu/aboutus/
http://www.jewishvirtuallibrary.org/jsource/biography/
moses.html
http://www.jewfaq.org/moshe.htm
http://www.religionfacts.com/judaism/practices/kosher.htm
http://www.jewfaq.org/kashrut.htm

Miracle 1
http://jewishencyclopedia.com/articles/9204-kapparah

Miracle 2
http://www.holocaust-education.dk/holocaust/ghettoer.asp
http://cghs.dadeschools.net/ib_holocaust2001/Ghettoes/
diet/diet.htm
http://chgs.umn.edu/museum/memorials/krakow/
http://www.sztetl.org.pl/en/city/zakliczyn/
http://www.holocaustresearchproject.org/ghettos/orderpolice.html

Miracle 3
http://www.case.edu/artsci/jdst/reviews/Mielec.htm
http://www.ushmm.org/wlc/en/article.php?ModuleId=10007056
http://www.megdal.com/Meyer/Testimony.htm

Miracle 4
http://www.ushmm.org/wlc/en/article.php?ModuleId=10005142
http://history1900s.about.com/library/holocaust/blarbeit.htm
http://www.ushmm.org/wlc/en/article.php?ModuleId=10005220
http://www.ushmm.org/wlc/en/article.php?ModuleId=10005189

http://www.yadvashem.org/yv/en/holocaust/about/05/
auschwitz_birkenau.asp

Miracle 5

http://www.nytimes.com/2013/03/03/sunday-review/the-
holocaust-just-got-more-shocking.html?pagewanted=all&_r=0
http://en.wikipedia.org/wiki/List_of_jet_aircraft_of_World_War_II
http://www.ushmm.org/wlc/en/article.php?ModuleId=10005537
http://b-29s-over-korea.com/German-Jets-In-WWII/German-
Jets-Inflicted-Severe-Damage-In-WWII_pg1.html

Miracle 6

http://www.timemoneyandblood.com/HTML/aircraft/
americanAircraft/aircraftAmerican.html
http://www.timemoneyandblood.com/HTML/aircraft/
britishAircraft/aircraftBritish.html
http://www.ipmsstockholm.org/magazine/1998/05/stuff_
eng_ww2incolor_airgerman.htm

Miracle 7

http://www.ushmm.org/wlc/en/article.php?ModuleId=10005162
http://www.yadvashem.org/odot_pdf/microsoft%20word%20
-%206260.pdf
http://books.google.com/books?id=GaAtH_yKTHAC&pg
=PA282&lpg=PA282&dq=death+march+holocaust+42+
days&source=bl&ots=oa0PspQlau&sig=_2Rdk8kfWRoX
N77SRLAzeQaJUnQ&hl=en&sa=X&ei=fVCmUY_eAs_
j4APYvYCYCQ&ved=0CFcQ6AEwBQ - v=onepage&q=death
march holocaust 42 dah

Miracle 8

http://search.ancestry.co.uk/cgi-bin/sse.dll?gl = 39&rank = 1&new = 1&so = 3&MSAV = 0&msT = 1&gss = ms_r_f-39&gsfn = Mendel&gsln = Neugut&msbpn__ftp = Poland&msbpn = 5183&msbpn_PInfo = 3-%7C0%7C1652381%7C0%7C5183%7C0%7C0%7C0%7C0%7C0%7C0%7C&sbo = 1&uidh = 000

private email to Arthur from Germany

http://www.ushmm.org/wlc/en/article.php?ModuleId = 10005129

http://postwargermany.wordpress.com/2012/10/02/black-market/

http://academic.udayton.edu/PMAC/Exercises/Exer13-1.htm

http://www.archives.gov/publications/prologue/2002/fall/berlin-black-market-1.html

http://www.theshipslist.com/ships/lines/americanscantic.shtml

http://en.wikipedia.org/wiki/Type_C4-class_ship

http://www.usmm.org/c4ships.html

Miracle 9

http://philadelphiaencyclopedia.org/archive/world-war-ii/

http://explorepahistory.com/story.php?storyId = 1-9-19

http://www.ourdocuments.gov/doc.php?flash = true&doc = 72

http://www.yadvashem.org/odot_pdf/Microsoft%20Word%20-%205817.pdf

http://academics.holycross.edu/files/Education/TCR_Memory_Test2.pdf

Miracle 10

http://www.aish.com/jl/l/m/48969841.html

http://www.myjewishlearning.com/life/Life_Events/Weddings/Liturgy_Ritual_and_Custom/Aufruf.shtml

http://www.chabad.org/library/article_cdo/aid/465165/jewish/The-Aufruf.htm

Epilogue

http://www.huffingtonpost.com/2013/04/26/as-holocaust-museum-turns-20-the-ranks-of-survivors-dwindle_n_3165667.html
http://www.algemeiner.com/2012/04/09/a-world-without-holocaust-survivors/

Made in the USA
Lexington, KY
24 October 2018